MW01201837

The Choice

The Choice

Best Regards

GERALD YANCEY

Gerald Yancey

Library of Congress Control Number:		2022914464
ISBN:	Hardcover	978-1-6698-4161-6
	Softcover	978-1-6698-4160-9
	eBook	978-1-6698-4159-3

Print information available on the last page.

Rev. date: 08/23/2022

To order additional copies of this book, contact:
Xlibris
844-714-8691
www.Xlibris.com
Orders@Xlibris.com
845067

CONTENTS

DEDICATION

To he who knows not . . .

INTRODUCTION

In writing this tale all attempts were made to be historically correct. Hopefully the reader will forgive any imprecision. Admittedly numerous redundancies will be discovered. Such resulted partly from the fact that over the years numerous writings were incorporated into the original manuscript and partly from desire to elaborate on certain themes.

Some say that truth is stranger than fiction. I have no point of view at this juncture. As such I am unable to express an opinion one way or the other. But in writing this narrative I have found that the truth is a lot more interesting. As an old fisherman my tales tend to get larger along with the size of the fish. Strenuous efforts were made to avoid this propensity but admittedly such impulses have been difficult to control.

Special thanks to Ruth Reese Carter who was responsible for maintaining close contact among all the members of St. Paul of the Cross Elementary.

My sincere thanks, and apologizes, go out to Stephanie Joldersma whose insight and patience contributed to the writing, re-writing and proof reading.

PROLOGUE

It was a chilly Thursday morning when God summoned my mom. He told her that one of her children must suffer. No real explanation was given. She would never understand and she knew it.

So mom went out to the fields and called for Mrs. Monday, who was chatting and laughing with a group of women. Lapozel Monday had once been our housekeeper and always said she would "walk the water." Her nickname was *Snow*. When asked why, she replied, "Because I was pure." Together they returned to God with their decision.

Prentiss was too important and was destined as a trailblazer in the fields of law and finance. Labat had troubles enough as it was. Mike was her sweetest child. So she couldn't bear the thought of the Lord's intent falling on his innocent brow.

That left me. I guess. Again I say it was a chilly Thursday morning. It happened en route from the emergency room at South Fulton Hospital where I was employed as a physician. An electric shock overcame me and my entire body felt as if it were on fire. I'd been listening to the Eric Clapton collection before it all happened. After wrestling the car to the side of the road, I slumped over the steering wheel. To this day I can still recall hearing *Knocking on Heaven's Door*, while in this painful state.

It turned out, I was struck with a very rare neurological disorder. But as the great Chuck Berry once said, "We will talk about that later." For now, however, I'm tired, on vacation, and seated at El Tucan Cafe in Puerto Barrios, Guatemala. My friend Stefan and our guide, Sonny from Monkey River Village, have gone ahead to shop. I couldn't keep up with them and all efforts to find a good novel to read have failed. Well, they do have pen and paper in Puerto Barrios. So from El Tucan Cafe, I begin this story.

CHAPTER 1

Johnnie Labat

I found the note on a Saturday. It was written in my mother's hand and was in essence a critique of her four sons. Prentiss was strong and mannerly. Labat was loving but had a bad temper. Mike was brilliant and was her gentlest baby. Gerald, myself, was a thief.

Slightly shocked, I looked at the note in dismay. I recovered quickly however and said, "You a lie", then promptly stole the note.

My mom always wanted a daughter though. When she became too overbearing, Mike would say, "I know you always wanted a girl, Clotilde, but I'm not her."

Clotilde Ouida Labat was her maiden name. But everybody knew her as Johnnie. Her family was from Bay St. Louis, Mississippi. The son of the grave digger was named Johnny and had a crush on mom when she was little. Her siblings teased her by calling his name over and over. After a while, she began to call herself the same name but with a different spelling. She always did have a fine sense of humor. My father was actually her second husband. She divorced her first husband within a year of their marriage. She was Catholic, however, and kept it a secret from her children until just prior to her death I knew anyway because Aunt Jean told me one day at age 14 while visiting in New Orleans. So when mom told each of her sons, one by one, she was surprised that I wasn't. We were raised on good ole Baltimore Catechism so I'd always known that something was fishy. I mean we would take communion every Sunday, but mom never did. So when I confronted Aunt Jean with this fact, she told me why.

Nacie or Aunt Inez arranged a deal with the Arch Bishop of New Orleans. Mom did not have to live with him anymore. They would call it an annulment but she couldn't take communion without special dispensation.

Mom told me later that her first husband only wanted her for her body. I never could figure out how that could be so bad. She was a beautiful woman in her day—slender, graceful, and with thick flowing locks of hair reminiscent of a crimson sunset. When she came to pick me up at Miss Scott's school, all the kids would say, "Who is that pretty lady?" Even first graders could appreciate a beautiful woman.

Miss Scott ran the school with her daughter, Miss Knox. It was Miss Knox who taught me how to teach myself. In those days, first, second, and third grades were all mixed. If you were advanced, you were able to do higher level work. That way no one was embarrassed, held back academically or socially isolated.

I will try to explain. For example, if you were advanced in first grade reading, math, or whatever to a higher level, you were allowed to do so to the second or third level. At the same time, you were not psychologically separated from your first grade friends. It was pure genius, really—whether by happenstance or intent.

Miss Knox had a real gift for teaching, and she discovered a certain technique from which students today could really benefit. At second grade level, you participated in the Current Events Bee. Each week you read the *Atlanta Journal & Constitution* and the Bee was held each Friday. The lady foreshadowed modern-day quiz shows. To this day at breakfast, we still read different sections of the paper among ourselves. And after breakfast, each talks about what he learned.

Somewhere along the line, the school deteriorated. I returned to Atlanta when my father was ill in 1986. The school was located near the corner of Ashby and Simpson roads where Charlie Sherman's filling station stood. Charlie pointed across the street as I paid him for the gasoline.

"Remember your old alma mater?" he would say. "Well, it's a crack house now." Several months later, I returned to Sherman's filling station. The old school was torn down.

CHAPTER II

Early Adventures

Mom was one of nine children. We knew of her parents as Papa Joe and Mama Noon. They passed long before my parents began to send us down to the Bay. We went each summer—Michael and I. Sometimes Labat came too.

Aunt Nan would take us crabbing. Uncle Vick would come over from New Orleans and teach us how to fish. Aunt Nacie would make us read in the backyard. Aunt Tennie and Aunt Sis would hide us from Aunt Nacie when we were tired of our studies.

Nacie was tough. She was principal in a New Orleans elementary school before the city's decline. I saw her call several teachers on the carpet in her office. It wasn't a very pretty sight. The kids at her school revered me with a certain awe. They couldn't believe that a relative to Nacie could be my age and still be alive.

Mom said that Nacie had been married once. Her husband was a doctor back in St. Louis. After Mama Noon died, there was no one to look over the children. The good doctor had no desire to live in Bay St. Louis. So Nacie left and became leader of the family.

Nan, Tennie, and Sis never married; but, Nan did have a boyfriend. His name was Ernie. Dad told me that when Ernie proposed to Nan, she passed out.

One summer mom arranged for Mike to fly from the Bay to New York City to be on the Howdy Doody Show. I couldn't believe that I wasn't going along as well and threw a fit. Mom said that I was too young to fly and Nacie offered to buy me ice cream. I took the ice cream and felt better almost immediately.

Later on, I realized why I could not go. Mike was much lighter in complexion than myself and even had blond curly locks. Mom was just tricking with the system.

I arrived at this conclusion during my teenage years while watching Mom's involvement with the Civil Rights Movement. She and Mike would frequent a segregated restaurant, Heron's, that specialized in lobster. Because they were so light in complexion, no one even questioned their entry.

Mom, over a year's time, charmed just about everyone from the owner to the scullion. Then one day she dressed me up and said, "We are taking you to Heron's." We entered, ate quietly, and left a large tip. We went there frequently afterwards and were always treated well.

Years later, Prentiss told me that Mom also used to slip into the White Citizen's Council, a white collar version of the KKK, and learned their plans. Johnnie was always tricking the system.

Early one evening, Uncle Vick and I went fishing on the bridge. He laid down his big cigar and informed me that he intended to make me into a "Bay Boy." At the time, I didn't understand. But I did know that whatever a "Bay Boy" was my relatives considered me far from perfect.

Now at a much later stage in life, I understand. A "Bay Boy" is simply a genuine human being who learns patience, tranquility, and kindness by living his life near the sea. I never cared much for hunting even though I could appreciate the chase which I found exhilarating. But after my first kill, I concluded at once that it wasn't for me. It just seemed to be inane. So I stuck to fishing and to this day have fished in waters far and wide. In my day, I have fished the waters of Nova Scotia, Cabo San Lucas, the Caribbean, and the Sea of Japan.

The best trip of my life took place at age 23. Mom had died and my father and I went to Nassau. Ian Bethel, Lollipops, and I took off for a one-week adventure in the waters off Eleuthera.

We mostly used snorkel, masks, and Hawaiian slings. By the fourth day, I was making 30 foot dives. You wouldn't believe the pressure at a mere 30 feet. We landed mostly grouper and lobster. At one time, we spied a shark trailing behind the boat. Ian decided to let the boat drift awhile in order to lose the shark. The boat drifted for about a mile in the current. Eventually, we started to fish again and I missed a hit on a large grouper.

As I came up, I saw the shark winding its way toward the stern. There was nothing I could do for Ian if he had not seen it. The shark tore off in a mad dash. I was located at least 20 feet from the port side. The next thing I can remember is that I found myself lying flat on my back with my flippered feet perched on the railings. I was looking up at the sun and noted another figure lying flat on my chest. It was Ian Bethel.

I spoke, "Ian . . . did you see that shark?"

Ian replied in a thick Bahamian accent, "What do you mean, Mon'? What do you think I am doing here on top of you!"

Well, that was enough to turn us around. We eventually found another location and continued our dives. It was adjacent to a medium-sized reef that I met The Black Dog. I met him once before at a younger age, but didn't expect to meet him in the calm waters of the Caribbean.

The Black Dog is my name for something that you fear as it has you in its grip. Mom used to tell us about a stray black dog that was roaming the neighborhood and biting small children. One day, there he was, growling and ready to pounce just lateral to our back porch. I was frozen in fear until my own dog, Waggy, appeared.

It was clear that they were friends. I could see Waggy before me and begging The Black Dog to spare my life. The Black Dog loved Waggy for the same reason that I did. He was good natured. After releasing a condescending growl, the animal trotted away and left me unharmed. I loved my dog Waggy very much.

But there I was in the Caribbean where The Black Dog found me again. This time it was in the form of a 5-foot barracuda. He was directly opposed to my face mask and slowly chopped and displayed some endless row of razor-sharp teeth.

They say that barracuda won't attack unless provoked. But I did not know whether this particular chap had kept up with common knowledge. So I slowly backed up to the reef and climbed out of the water.

I don't really know whether you have ever seen a reef or not, but in essence, a reef is razor sharp. Slowly, I walked on top with only my flippers protecting my feet. It must have taken me some 45 minutes to walk a mere 12 steps. After doing so, I jumped into a pocket of water that would support my height and weight. Well, there I was in this small cove that essentially was a lobster nest.

I couldn't count the number of antenna that projected from beneath the numerous rocks. I proceeded to load up my sling and commenced to fire. After kill number 10, I spotted Ian off in the boat. He and Lollipops came over to help. By the time we went home, we netted over 30 lobster. We also picked Wilkes off the reef and gathered the plentiful conch that lay on the ocean floor.

After the trip, my brother Prentiss and I were talking about the movie *Jaws*. He mentioned that after I saw it I wouldn't be so adventurous. I did, in fact, see the movie. It doesn't compare to the real thing.

Many years have elapsed since my early age adventures. I really don't know if I ever became a "Bay Boy." I do know this though. When Aunt Nan was dying, she commanded that "My Boy" appear regardless of my own ill health. As much as it tired me, I complied.

CHAPTER III

Seventeen Forty Part One

It was a magical place. 1740 Simpson Rd NW was built by my father, Dr. P.Q. Yancey, some time in the early 50's. At that time, it was semi-rural and few understood why he wanted to move so far away from Moreland Avenue which at that time was where many members of the Afro- American middle-class set-up house.

I never questioned his motives, but did question why he chose to move to Atlanta as opposed to the sandy shores of Savannah. He responded, "For political protection". It wasn't until years later that I realized what he meant. Morehouse College, Spellman, Atlanta University, Clark and Morris Brown were centers of higher learning for the "colored race". As things evolved, blacks, whites and Jews began to form coalitions.

By the time I completed my senior year at the Marist School, my parents were in direct contact with MLK, Jr. and Sr., Mayor Ivan Allen, Julian Bond, Senator Leroy Johnson, attorney Henry DeGive, future Georgia Supreme Court Justice Charlie Weltner, Fulton County District Attorney Louis Slaton, the Passionist fathers, the sisters of St. Ambrose, and Bishop Francis Edward Hyland of the Diocese of Atlanta only to name a few. So if trouble was a brewing...as it always is...we had a network of political support.

I do not wish to stray too far afield from the original theme. As such, I will attempt to describe the physical characteristics of our home at 1740. 1740 was located between Richardson Road to the east and the winding Whittaker Road to the west. The house stood above a high sloping hill and the foundation was based in granite rock. As the driveway neared the top of the hill it turned into an oval that circumscribed a middle area of bushes, grasses and trees. Viewing the house from Simpson Road on the left was the family of Fleetwood Roberts. As the property enveloped Whittaker Road on the right, the nearest house just behind 1740 housed the family of Andrew and William Frank Harper. Upon ascending the driveway, the left side was heavily thickened with trees mostly oak, hickory and pine. The right side was essentially clear and contained a small area that descended into a small valley. We often referred to this valley as "The Pit". Just above the pit was a tennis court and beneath that was a cleared area with a gate that exited onto Whittaker Road.

The house itself consisted of four bedrooms, an entranceway, a living room, a kitchen and laundry area, a den, and a screened in porch in the rear. A large backyard also existed with a patio as well as a large hand-crafted barbecue pit that was made of solid stone.

I should mention that in the area just beneath the tennis court that we used for a football field there also existed a wooden basketball goal. Somewhere along the line my good friends Clifford Lowe and Frank Booker and I removed the goal from the lower area where the playing area consisted of dirt, up to the tennis court where the playing area consisted of asphalt instead. In writing this narrative I have attempted to do so in chorological order and to be as accurate as possible. However, given old age and its accompanying maladies, I cannot warrant either. So, without further ado, I begin to tell the tale of 1740 to the best of my ability.

First Sight

The first thing I recall seeing upon gaining a sense of sight was my mother, Clothilde "Johnnie" Yancey, as she exited the threshold leading from the den to the dining room. The view was dim and colors were barely discernable. I also recognized the knotty pine walls along with the stacks of bookshelves that held an abundance of material which later on came to be known to me as books and magazines.

My second recollection was that of our maid, Mrs. Parks, who carried me often on her right hip with my chest and abdomen curved inwards. As such, I suspect that this method of toting lead me to view the world in a manner somewhat different from many.

Often, I woke up on Saturday morning to accompany my father as he took his AM coffee. On one occasion I formed a cape from discarded bed linen and wrote a large "S" on the back. As my father had his back turned and was looking out the window towards the yard, I tied the cape around my neck, shut my eyes, and leapt from the counter spread-eagle. As you might imagine, I did not get very far. So, as I rose weeping in a pool of blood flowing from my upper chin, my father quickly turned around and ascertained the situation.

After being stitched up by my father he asked me what I was thinking. I replied that I thought I could fly like Superman. Actually, I forgot all about the event until last year when my dentist, Dr. Keith Kitchens asked me about the scar just beneath my lower lip. I told him the story. He chuckled then proceeded to stick me with a hypodermic needle to numb the planned dental field. Needless to say, I shut my eyes again.

The Black Dog

My first dog was named Waggy. He was a moderate-sized white mutt. He was intelligent as hell and as playful and rambunctious as myself. As such he became one of my favorite companions in life.

One Saturday morning as a I was wandering outdoors, I came across "The Black Dog" face to face. He was known as such throughout the neighborhood as mean spirited and vicious yet had not been caught. Needless to say, I was quite frightened as he growled and barred his teeth. I was still a small child and felt as though he was preparing to pounce. Immediately at his side appeared Waggy. Oddly enough they appeared to communicate as I watched Waggy arguing and finally convincing The Black Dog to let me alone as I was a good and kind master. Grudgingly, The Black Dog sulked away but gave me a vicious glance that seemed to say, "Lucky you". Naturally I was grateful to Waggy and promptly fed him one his favorite dishes, to wit, a can of Campbell's chicken noodle soup.

Shooting James Roberts

While growing up I discovered the joys of climbing whether it be trees, rock formations or even upon the roof of our home at 1740. On one occasion I attempted to conquer a slender pine tree that was located just next to the fence that separated the Yancey property from that of the Roberts. I do not recall exactly what happened. However, I do recall waking up in my bedroom sometime in the evening and seeing cuts and sores on both legs.

As I was looking forward to seeing "Heidi" on television, I heard the sounds of the beginning of the film emanating from my parents' room. I arose immediately and my mother informed me that Mrs. Roberts found me on the ground beneath the tree, picked me up and carried me inside the house. I had been unconscious for at least eight hours! As a youngster I could easily shrug things off and without a second thought took a seat and enjoyed the film.

But that was not the end of my encounter with the Roberts family. James and I were the best of play pals and enjoyed each other's company immensely. One day however, he had in his possession a BB gun and was using a tree for target practice. I asked if I could play with it for a while. He complied and passed it over the fence. Lacking an immediately desirable target, I found one in James!

First, I aimed the gun at his head, but decided that was too dangerous. Then I considered his chest, but finally chose to target his legs. As I hit him on the left calf he howled in pain. Immediately I threw the gun back over the fence and hightailed it for the house.

I never heard of a complaint to my parents and suspect that either James kept mum or that the Roberts family decided to let the matter pass.

Some thirty-five years later when I was a practicing emergency room physician at South Fulton Hospital, James was admitted for a laceration to his right eyelid suffered during a car accident. Hiding behind a surgical cap and mask, I proceeded, along with the aid of a nurse, to cleanse the eye of glass and other debris. After sewing the eyelid up, I revealed myself. We had a joyful reunion and planned to have lunch soon. I also informed him that there would be no charge as I saw this as a way to repay him the harm I caused in shooting him in the leg. He paused, but admitted that he did not recall the event.

Well… I did, and we did have lunch and I made certain that I paid the entire tab. However, to this day, I still think I remain eternally in his debt.

CHAPTER IV

Seventeen Forty-
Respite Part-Two

Fifty-three BB's and a Slingshot

As it turned out, this was not my last experiment with my fascination with BB's. One day I purchased a handheld slingshot from Cooper's Drug Store located on Simpson Road just a few blocks east. I also purchased a pack of BB's. After loading the BB's in the leather slingshot pouch, I took aim and fired at several coke bottles that I had lined up on a wooden bench.

After running out of bottles, I found several unused window panes lying behind the garage that were left over from some previous home project. Quickly I ran out of window panes to shoot at as well. So, what was left to shoot at I thought. My attention then turned to the windows of our home which numbered approximately 53. I then proceeded to put a BB hole in nearly all windows until I came to my senses. Several days later my father noted the BB holes in some of the windows and then proceeded to inspect the entire home. He found BB holes along with BB's in nearly every window in the house.

Automatically my father assumed that the insult was inflicted by our neighbors "Pig" and James Season who lived just to the south and were known for being skilled marksmen with their BB guns.

He then directed my mother to call the police. As she was calling, I came to her side and tried to draw her attention. "Oh, Mom, I started." "Quiet, Gerald. I'm calling the police", she responded.

"Ah…Mom. It was me".

She slowly returned the phone to the receiver and just stared at me in disbelief. I then recalled what happened and informed her that "Pig" and James had no part in the matter.

Slowly she grasped me by the arm and lead me to the basement stairway, locked the door and put the key in her purse. Some thirty minutes later I heard my father drive off to work. I think it was not until around 10:00 p.m. that I heard the door unlock. My mother told me to promptly go to bed.

I never heard it discussed again. Years later however, Lauren Young, daughter of Whitney and Margaret Young, informed me that my parents, being fearful of safety issues concerning the family, sought advice of the Young family in regard to finding psychiatric consultation for their youngest son Gerald.

Whitney responded with his usual wry humor, "The boys not insane, Johnnie. He's just crazy!" Several years ago, I was contacted by Deborah Patrick, the new owner of 1740, to come and see what she had found. Upon entering the house, she quickly escorted me to the rear of the living room where it was adjacent to the opening of the screened in porch. There to the lower left panel I spied a small hole with a BB resting snugly on the base of the inside frame.

Firebombs, Tractors and Roller-skates

Somewhere along the line I discovered by placing a garden hose inside of my father's car that I could create a suction then promptly drop the hose into a mason jar to collect gasoline. After sealing the mason jar, I would cut a hole in it and stick a cloth wick inside. Thereafter,

I would carry the family trash down to the aforementioned pit, douse the trash with gasoline and then light the wick of my newly created firebomb a/k/a "Molotov cocktail". I would then proceed to throw the glass jar against the rocks which promptly exploded and light-up the trash below all with one glee inspiring explosion.

On several occasions I would use the syphoned gasoline to fill-up a self-powered hand-held tractor that my father had purchased from Sears & Roebuck. In the wee hours of the morning I would fill up the tractor with gasoline, slyly let the tractor roll down hill and attach my roller skates to both shoes. Thereafter I would start up the tractor and proceed to ride about the sleepy neighborhood feeling like Ben Hur on roller skates. My path would lead me up the high hill of Richardson Road with a quick turn to the right descending upon the cured Whittaker Road then returning to Simpson and performing a U-turn whereby I re-entered the driveway and calmly parked the tractor in place.

While performing this stunt on my last occasion, my music instructor, Wesley Jackson, had risen early from bed to get the mail. He looked at me and I could see that his eyes were dilated like saucers. I quickly placed my fingers over my lips in an effort to plead that he remain silent. As he never reported my zany adventure to my parents, I decided to cease and desist in this endeavor.

However, I did not cease in regard to creating the Molotov mason jar cocktail. Eventually this practice caught up with me. One morning as I was syphoning gasoline, I was too slow to shift the hose to the mason jar. As you might guess, I inadvertently swallowed a large amount of gasoline.

Luckily, I was a boy scout at that time. After consulting my scout manual, I promptly drank copious amounts of milk while belching gasoline fumes at the same time. After what seemed like an eternity, I felt much better. During dinner my mother inquired, "Who drank up all the milk, and what's that horrible smell?" Naturally, I remained silent.

Guitar for Rent

As previously mentioned, my music instructor was Wesley Jackson. He taught me to play the Ukulele while at the same time he taught my brother Labat to play the electric guitar. Eventually we both lost interest and our various instruments lay in our closets and accumulated dust.

One day however, Mr. Broom, our family yard man, asked if he could rent out the guitar, which belonged to Labat, to play at Sunday services. I promptly complied and rented out the guitar for a fee of $3.00 per day. Now at $ .25 per comic book, $3.00 translated into quite a collection of Superman, Green Lantern, Aquaman, Spiderman and Magnus the Robot Fighter comics.

Eventually Labat found out and complained. "Gerald, you are renting out my guitar without my permission!" My only reply as I recall was "Huh?" I quickly terminated my guitar rental business with Mr. Broom and turned to other endeavors.

Thermometer Readings

On occasion, I really did not want to go to school as I wanted to spend the day with my mother helping out with shopping and basically just enjoying her companionship. In that regard, I would complain of feeling ill and my mother would promptly place a mercury thermometer under my tongue, then return approximately three minutes later for the reading. At that point I would take the thermometer and place it next to the lightbulb so as to increase my temperature to at least 101. My mother reported the findings to my father who after examining me thought I merely had contracted some form of virus and needed to be placed on his favorite aspirin to break the fever.

Miraculously I would feel much better sometime around 1:00 when it was time for my mother to perform her daily errands. After my father returned home for dinner, he would swear by the miracle drug known as Empirin compound. On one occasion I held the thermometer to the lightbulb for too long a period. I looked at the thermometer and the temperature was a whopping and suspiciously unbelievable 104! I busily shook it down to around 101.5 and promptly reinserted it into my mouth just seconds prior to my mother entering the room. Thereafter I discontinued the practice as no doubt my parents would soon discover the hoax if I continued to push my luck.

The Blue Tattoo

I previously mentioned going to Cooper's Drugstore which was only a few blocks away from my home. Next to Cooper's Drugstore a Jewish man by the name of Mr. Hersh ran a grocery store. We often did our mother's shopping at that neighborhood grocery and Mr. Hersh was always kind and helpful. One day however, Mr. Hersh was wearing a short-sleeve shirt and I noticed a blue tattoo on his left inner forearm that contained a set of numbers. I promptly asked him what was meant by the blue tattoo. At that point Mr. Hersh looked down and I noticed that a few tears were streaming down his eye. My mother promptly paid for the groceries ushered me into the car and explained that Mr. Hersh was incarcerated in a German concentration camp during Word War II because he was Jewish.

At first I did not quite understand. In fact, even when I read about the Holocaust in World History class somewhere between 3rd and 4th grade, I recall one or two lines that mentioned the persecution of the Jews in Germany. I still could not fathom that 5-6 million Jews could have been killed so mercilessly by anyone. In fact, I do not think that the Holocaust ever struck me as being a true historical event until I saw a film depicting dead bodies and mass graves while attending a special summer program designed to expose college level course work to high school students that was sponsored by Morehouse and Spellman Colleges.

CHAPTER V

Seventeen Forty Respite-
Part Three

The Ricochet Rock

As I mentioned earlier, "The Pit" was another magical place that I explored for its numerous nooks and crannies along with its rock formations. One day I decided to create an escape route whereby I could strike one of my brothers, run along a pre-created path along the rim of the pit and then slide down the bottom on a stack of leaves. I accomplished this to a certain measure of success on at least two occasions. However, upon the third as I struck my brother Labat, ran along the escape path, and slid down to the bottom of the pit and continued to run. Labat then hurled a rock at me that missed me by a mile. However, the rock did glance off a tree to my left and like a billiard, struck me on my left forehead.

As the blood gushed copiously, Labat begged that I stop crying because mom no doubt would administer a strong whipping. Cognizant of my own deviant behavior, we were able to put together a plan for our mutual protection. Labat gave me his t-shirt which I applied to the left side of my forehead. We informed my mom that I was balancing on a stone wall at the base of the hill, slipped and Labat saw me and staunched the blood with his t-shirt. Luckily for both of us she swallowed the story, expressed her pride in Labat's quick thinking and sent me packing to my father's office to get my forehead stitched up. I still bear the scar on my left forehead to this day.

My daredevil adventures did not end there and I continued to engage in reckless endeavors which often resulted in my father having to sew up one laceration after the other.

Finally, my father informed me that the next time I cut myself he was not going to give me anesthesia and would sew me up without any type of pain relief whatsoever. To be honest, I did not believe him. However, that faithful day eventually arrived. I was cutting onions with a new onion slicer but had my right palm on the wrong side of the unprotected end of the slicer. Naturally, I sliced into my right palm. As I held my right palm underneath cold water and pressed on the wound with my left, I saw my father turn and walk away in disgust. I then exclaimed to myself, "He doesn't love me at all!"

My father returned after approximately two minutes with his black doctor bag in hand, pulled out his suture kit and promptly began to sew up the wound. I asked him before he started, was he not going to give me something for pain. He said "No. I warned you over and over and this time you will get no local anesthetic from me". I winced during the entire procedure which as I recall required at least four stiches. I still bear this particular scar on my right palm. But my father's approach did in fact work. I cannot say that I ceased my daredevil adventures, but I was more careful in their execution. I guess every scar has a story and I am certain that the reader can attest to that fact.

Sonny Epps

Sonny Epps was a bully. He was tall and strong and for unexplained reasons he was quite mean spirited. In the neighborhood surrounding Simpson Road, Whittaker Road and Detroit Avenue there were at least three or four basketball goals in various backyards. Sonny's basketball goal was designed far ahead of its time in that the net was made out of chain link. Scoring would give off a tremendous sound, especially when you hit "Nothing but the bottoms". However, very few of us went over to play at Sonny's court because as I stated before, he was mean spirted and bullysome.

One day I ventured to said area and enjoyed shooting hoops and listening to the sound of the links. Sonny came outside and as I greeted him he quickly gut punched me in the abdomen. After that I never ventured to his backyard as nor did any of my other playmates. However, one day Labat and Sonny got into it and a fight ensued. A few days later I heard of the event and it spread like wildfire throughout the neighborhood that Labat had beat up Sonny Epps. Naturally we were all very proud that Labat, like David, had defeated the giant Goliath also known as Sonny Epps. It was only about three years ago when I questioned Labat as to how he accomplished such a feat. He then confessed, "Sonny slipped and I grabbed him in a headlock and wouldn't let go until he pleaded for mercy".

"So you mean to tell me that you beat up him because he slipped?" Labat reiterated that not only did Sonny Epps slip, but he held on to his head in a hammerlock for dear life until Sonny finally gave in and pleaded to be released. Needless to say, Sonny never forgave Labat for such an ignominious and wildly applauded neighborhood defeat.

The Werewolf

Often times our neighborhood community would attend movies at the Ashby Street theater. The biggest draws were sword and sandal movies such as Ben Hur, The Ten Commandments, The Robe, Demetrius and the Gladiators and Solomon and Sheba. Every Sunday during this period of racially segregated movie theaters the Ashby Street theater would be packed with a swarm of black kids eager to enjoy the miracle of the big screen along with hot dogs, popcorn and soda pop.

On one Sunday my mother was in the process of carrying Michael and myself to drop us off at the Ashby Street theater to see a particular movie. Upon arriving at the crest of Richardson Road, my mother asked me if I had done my homework for Monday. I lied and said yes. She then asked Michael if he had done his homework. Now I knew I was in trouble. because Michael was incapable of lying. He then told mom that he did not do his homework at which point she turned her head, struck him on the legs as he was sitting in the back seat and then crashed into an oncoming car. Luckily no one was hurt. Given that, she promptly drove us both back home. As Michael proceeded to do his homework in his room, I quickly scurried down to the basement and completed mine.

On one Sunday mom dropped us off at the Ashby Street theater for a double header. The first movie was "Forbidden Planet" and the second was "The Werewolf". Michael and I were both afraid when we arrived home. Michael feared the creature from the Id in "Forbidden Planet". I feared the werewolf. In a game of psych out, I portrayed the monster from the Id and Michael portrayed the werewolf. Instantly I gave in as I was more afraid of the werewolf than he was of the monster from the Id. That night as it was time to go to sleep, I could not rest.

My reason was that the werewolf was coming to get me. As Labat and I shared the same room, I thought to myself Labat could not protect me from the werewolf. Neither could my father nor mother protect me. Michael certainly couldn't protect me. However, the only one in the family who could protect me from the werewolf was my older brother Prentiss . Thereafter, I immediately left my room and hopped in the bed with him. Naturally, he was irate and ordered me to get out of his bed. I refused. I explained to him he was the only one who could protect me from the werewolf. Instantly mom came to inquire what all the commotion was about. I informed mom, "The werewolf is coming to get me... the werewolf is coming to get me. The only one who can protect me from the werewolf is Prentiss!" My mom chuckled a bit and said, "Let him spend at least one night".

Prentiss grumbled but at least I knew I was safe from being attacked by the werewolf that night. No longer afraid of being under attack, I spent the next night sleeping in my own room with Labat who was my roommate.

Blood and Basketball

Somewhere in time, as stated before, my friends Clifford Lowe and Frank Booker and myself decided to remove the wooden basketball goal that was located below the tennis court up to the tennis court itself and post it in the grass behind the serving line. An open invitation was sent out to all comers and thus included the Washington Park, Mosely Park, Turner High, Detroit Avenue and Dixie Hills neighborhoods. This project worked out very well for a number of months and on any given Saturday, the tennis court was full of at least twenty to thirty kids waiting in line to compete in the "Three on Three Basketball League".

Whenever my father came home from work sometime around 4:00 p.m. I told all the kids to stand up and wave and holler, "Hey Dr. Yancey". My father at the top of the hill was always amazed to see so many black children playing basketball peacefully and happily on the newly formed basketball court within the asphalt tennis court. Unfortunately, this seemingly happy and harmonious arrangement would not last for long.

On one Saturday as I exited the house to play basketball with my compatriots I noticed that the entire situation had turned violent. Tony Hill and Warren Dallas had gotten into an argument over who knows what. As I cleared through the surrounding spectators, I saw Tony holding Warren by his ears and banging his head on the asphalt which was now red from blood that was spewing out of the posterior scalp of Warren's head. Immediately I instructed Frank and Clifford to assist me in breaking the two up. Further I shouted, "You guys have got to beat it. Dr. Yancey is on the way home!"

Well that got everybody's attention and as all involved held my father in high regard, they quickly scattered from whence they came. Clifford and Frank then escorted Warren Dallas to Grady Hospital to get his laceration sewed up. After the coast was clear, I proceeded to clean up the blood. Needless to say, the all comers invitation was nullified. Approximately a month thereafter we instituted a by invitation only arrangement whereby no more than twelve invitees who were known to be well-behaved were allowed to come and play basketball at the court located at 1740.

CHAPTER VI

Seventeen Forty
Respite-Part Four

The Thunderbird

After obtaining his driver's license my brother Labat was permitted to have free access to a now classic Ford Thunderbird vehicle. It was a true beauty. At that time, it contained brand new state of the art equipment such as power steering, power brakes, air conditioning and a radio which are now thought merely standard. The front two seats were bucket seats as opposed to the usual bench style. The leather interior, plush carpeting as well as the streamlined exterior all glistened in a pearly white finish.

For his 16th birthday mom and dad threw him a surprise party in our aforementioned basement that was once my prison. I was only 12 at the time and truly enjoyed watching the older kids dancing the twist, the mashed potato, the monkey, the Madison and many of the other rave dances that had filtered their way from the industrial cities of Detroit, Chicago and New York City. Around 10:00 that night my father had just returned from work and walked downstairs to view the situation. He held up his hand between songs and asked, "Labat, what is the Thunderbird doing parked in the tennis court?"

Of course, we were all stunned and for a while were immobilized. Slowly we all lined up and went upstairs through the foyer and out the front door to gasp at a truly incredible sight. The Thunderbird had rolled down the hill over the grass and crashed into the right corner of the tennis court which was now caved in from the right side towards the center. I stood next to Labat who obviously was more shocked than I was. Slowly the kids all milled out, hopped in their cars, and departed the scene.

One said, "Goodbye, Labat".

Another said, "Happy birthday, Labat".

A third said, "See ya later, Labat".

As it turned out, Labat had forgotten to place the gear shift in the park position and left it in neutral. So slowly, as gravity would have it, the car eventually rolled down the hill, somehow missing all other parked cars, and smashed into the court. Needless to say, the entire family went to bed earlier than usual and over a period of about a week, picked up the pieces so to speak and eventually the tennis court was restored to its earlier pristine condition. Much to my joy, the basketball post only suffered a few scratches.

Juanita Cox

One day after arriving home from Marist, I entered the house to find my mother distraught and in tears. She informed me that a girl by the name of Juanita Cox called her up just hours ago and said that I had gotten her pregnant and that she and her mother would come over to talk to the family at 5:00 p.m. As Michael was nearby, he spoke up to say, "Mom, Gerald has never even had sex".

I replied, "What do you mean I've never even had sex! How would you know, Michael? Oh, and by the way, Mom, I've never had sex. This is some hoax created by some girl just designed to get you upset."

My mother continued to cry and asked me to remain there until 5:00. I refused knowing that no one was ever going to show up. In fact, I had a plan. I contacted my dear friend Kathy Connely to canvas the Washington High School area. Tony Axam covered Harper High. Beverley Brown covered Turner High. Judy Dennard covered Price High and Bill Cannon covered Drexel High.

Around 6:00 we found out the name of the perp and discussed what action we should take. Finally, through our network, we were able to come to an agreement that the girl was to be shunned until she graduated. Needless to say, this approach was quite effective particularly when applied to a high school teenage girl. Juanita Cox…as she slyly called herself…had violated the cardinal rule of the neighborhood. You just don't mess with anyone's mother.

A few months later my mother approached me and said, "Now Gerald, I'm not saying that it is ok for you to have sex with a girl. I am only saying that Leroy Johnson told his son Michael that if he ever did have sex with a girl to make sure that he used a rubber. But I'm not saying that you have permission to have sex". At this point, I will leave it to the reader to figure that one out for himself.

You're the Only Doctor Who Gets His Fee

Marietta Dockery and her husband, Dr. "Big George" Dockery lived in a high-rise condo somewhere around 125th Street in New York City. George was a dentist and served many of the celebrities of Afro-American descent in Manhattan. Thus, when some came to perform or visit Atlanta, Marietta naturally being great friends with my parents would plan for one celebrity or another to visit 1740 either for breakfast, lunch, dinner or even to spend the night. My brother Prentiss had an early recollection of waking up early one morning and finding a gigantic black man chowing down on a barbecue spare rib for breakfast. His name was Joe Lewis.

The first celebrity I recall was Leslie Uggams as she had gained fame when her biggest brake came on the Lawrence Welk's show. She also became a regular on "Sing-Along with Mitch" produced by a starring conductor, Mitch Miller. Most recently, I recalled seeing Leslie perform as Blind Al in the movie "Deadpool 2".

Lena Horne spent two nights with us as she was performing at what I think was the Atlanta Civic Center. During dinner my brother Michael asked her if she would perform his favorite, "The Zoo". We attended a performance that evening and she performed her usual melodious song and ballads. When called on for an encore she stated, "I would like to dedicate this song to a little boy by the name of Michael Yancey, who asked me to sing it especially for him". She then went on to sing the song that Michael requested, to wit, "The Zoo". Surprisingly it excited the audience so much that everyone stood up, clapped and cheered. She received more applause by singing "The Zoo" than she did all the other songs combined.

Sugar Ray Robinson also came to visit us and to have dinner. As my mother prepared the meal, she asked me to drive Sugar Ray and his wife Ray around Atlanta and show them the town. I happily complied and while driving noticed that Sugar Ray who was sitting in the rear behind his wife was very quiet and kept sniffing from time to time. I looked over at his wife Ray and questioned in a silent gesture that was meant to say, "What is that all about?" She looked back at me and winked. Later on, she explained to me that from his years of boxing, Sugar Ray had become punch drunk. So that explained why he rarely spoke and often sniffed as if he was still in the ring.

I think I was in my first year at Penn Med when my brother Prentiss invited me to meet he and the entire American Basketball Players Association for a scheduled meeting in Nassau, Bahamas. There I met Artis Gilmore and most notably Julius Irving among others. After the meeting, the group returned to Atlanta and held a picnic in the backyard of our good friend, former NBA basketball player, Jimmy Washington. After much begging and cajoling, I convinced several of the players to join in a game of three on three.

Grudgingly, they agreed, just to shut "The Kid" up. Upon gaining possession of the ball, I immediately attacked the rim. Surprisingly, I felt myself bouncing off what felt like an invisible electromagnetic field, and much to my chagrin, found that I no longer had the ball in my possession. Of course, the professional players cracked up laughing. Finally, after gaining possession once more, I went to the far-right corner and took my favorite trick shot, which was a nothing but the bottoms swoosh, only inches away from the out of bounds marker. Boom...I scored a two pointer. They all laughed and one stated, "Now can we go eat?"

The next day the group came to our house at 1740 and were treated to a hardy breakfast in our large dining room that consisted of scrambled eggs, pancakes, a stack of porkchops, country ham, corn on the cobb and cracklin bread. I don't think that any of them had ever enjoyed such a sumptuous breakfast as they inhaled the meal as though they were going to the electric chair.

As the table was being cleared off, my father entered the room and asked, "Which one of you is Dr. J?"

Julius Irving then stood up and said, "I am Dr. Yancey".

My father replied, "You're the only doctor who gets his fee".

A hearty laughter broke out as Julius Irving took a bow and as my father slowly exited the room.

Four Billy Goats Gruff

There were four Billy Goats Gruff who resided along with their parents at 1740. One day they had to cross a bridge that spanned a stream to graze in the meadow beyond. The first Billy Goat was named Gerald. As he crossed the bridge, a gigantic troll jumped out of the water and stated, "I'm going to gobble you up!"

Gerald Billy Goat replied, "Don't eat me. Eat my brother Michael. He's coming next, and he's very sweet".

The troll replied, "Oh boy, I like sweet".

As Michael Billy Goat crossed the bridge the troll jumped up and showed "I'm going to gobble you up!"

Michael Billy Goat replied, "Don't eat me. Eat my brother Labat. He's right behind me, and he's bitter-sweet".

The troll then replied, "Oh my, bitter-sweet is even better".

As Labat Billy Goat crossed the bridge, the troll jumped up and screamed, "I'm going to gobble you up!"

Labat Billy Goat replied, "Don't eat me. Eat my brother Prentiss. He's coming right behind me. He's big and chocolatey".

The troll replied, "Oh boy, I love chocolate".

As Prentiss Billy Goat crossed the bridge, the troll jumped up and exclaimed, "I'm going to gobble you up!"

Prentiss Billy Goat shook his head, lowered both horns and launched into the troll at full throttle. The blow broke the troll's jaw and sent him howling in pain back into the stream below.

After crossing the bridge, Prentiss Billy Goat looked at his younger three Billy Goats Gruff and said, "What the hell was that all about?"

The three younger Billy Goats Gruff merely scampered off towards the meadow land singing, "Hippity hoppity, hippity hoppity, dippity, dippity doo!"

CHAPTER VII

St. Paul Remembered

In third grade, Mom decided to send me to St. Paul of the Cross Elementary School. It was run by the Sisters of St. Joseph headquartered in Baden Pennsylvania and the Passionist Order of Priests. Father Emmanuel Trainer served as the First Pastor and celebrated the first Mass on January 20, 1955 in the Birch Room of McLendon Hospital. Sister Mildred Ildephonse was obviously the Queen of the Universe and Father Dennis Walsh, our second Pastor, was the King. The parish also had a Boy Scout troop that was run by Retired Army Sergeant Major Milton Jones.

I think it was Sister Malcolm who played an important role in my personal development. I was already a top student due to the efforts of Ms. Knox. As I mentioned before, Miss Knox taught me how to teach myself. I did have some problems with my physical development, however. As quietly a secret as it can be kept, among boys at least, that can be a serious problem. Men must know how to fight and I was a physical coward.

One day Sister Malcolm called me into a room. She asked me to do some research for the track team. Upon completion, I informed her that the winner of a race was the one whose torso first crossed the tape. Most of the guys on the team didn't know what a torso even was. They knew how to run, however. She then informed me that she wanted me to play the position of catcher on the school softball team. With a gulp, I complied

My first game was a disaster. I went zero for four, dropped flies, and could not possibly throw to second base. Maceo Boozer—a real catcher—complained bitterly. Billy Bradley would shake his head in disgust. Amaryllis Grogan, a superb female athlete, informed me, "You can't hit or you can't catch. I can't remember which one it is." I think she had a crush on me.

My second game was a little better. Ken Gordon from Our Lady of Lourdes went out of his way to clip me on a run from third base. His own principal, Father McKeever, sent a messenger over. "Gerald," be began, "Father says next time he tries that, kick him in the teeth." Well, that was encouraging. At least the opposite side had a coach who believed in me or so I thought. He probably believed in fair play more. But the lesson was clear. To enforce my rights, I had to be willing to fight for them.

After that incident, I began to drill and practice. I would throw a tennis ball against the front steps located at the entrance to our beautiful home on 1740 Simpson Road. The return was unpredictable and so I learned how to field a ball in play. The better I became, the harder I threw and the closer I got. Then I found batting cages located near the old state fairgrounds and practiced batting.

By the time my third game came around, I was a different player. I scored twice and committed no errors. I never will forget that game. It was against the Collier Heights team. I will never forget it because during that game, Horace Grogan hit a homer that broke the third floor window of the school.

Sister Malcolm saw potential in me and patiently waited until I added the necessary ingredient—aggression. It was then when I began to consider the concept of myself as student-athlete. It was merely a concept at that stage, however. The realization of that notion would not occur until much later in life.

St. Paul was spawned in an attempt to spread Catholicism among the colored population of the day. It was a magnificent alliance between Anglo-American Christianity and people of African descent. I had no idea of how powerful this alliance would become. None of us foresaw the Civil Rights movement in its full flower, the election of John F. Kennedy, the assassination of Martin Luther King, Jr., or the birth of rock music from the womb of the Blues.

These were tranquil, productive days. Segregation was still in place but Black men neither attacked whites nor considered suicide. Black people back then were fun-loving, creative, and striving. And the blight of white powder was nowhere to be found in our communities. I shouldn't really say "Black" because back then we were colored. We were really ashamed of being called Black. The word Negro was just Spanish for Black, and that was alright. When Stokely Carmichael & Company began to use the term more freely the connotation of inferiority was soon to be erased.

It made sense I told mom one night, "Call yourself what you are afraid of being called. That way what you once feared becomes your best weapon." Mom got the idea. It was a political notion. It had no real basis in the world of genetics or history. It was politics plain and simple. I mean who could understand any better than my mom! After all, she had changed her own name from Clotilde to Johnnie.

At St. Paul, the mass was still celebrated in Latin. Most of the guys became Altar Boys and could speak, pray, and sing in Latin. Gregorian chant was an awesome mystery. I still miss it and think that the Catholic Church should return to that form of expression.

At times, it appears that somewhere in space, there is a large hole in the universe. Through that hole, I believe, all the magic and mystery of life slowly leaks. If we look real hard on the other side of that leak, we might find among other lost treasures, The Cantate and the Stabat Mater.

Milton Jones was our scoutmaster. He developed at least three of us into Eagle Scouts. We also had five members to receive the Ad Altare Dei medal.

The entire troop turned out for both occasions. My brother Michael and I were members of both groups. Several years ago I searched high and low for my Ad Altare Dei medal but to no avail. Eventually I made contact with proper authorities who directed me to meet with them at St. George Village, a retirement community sponsored by the Catholic Church. So we met at St. George and the award was re-presented to myself and Mike. It was bestowed upon us by then Arch Bishop Wilton Gregory-currently Cardinal Wilton Gregory.

Later on, I began to see that the striving for excellence was inextricably woven with the desire to receive the honor itself. Pride in one's work was essential to achieve. In order to achieve, the work must have quality. As with any fine accomplishment, the ends and the means are inseparable. Stated differently, the product is simply a reflection of the procedure while the procedure is reflected in the product itself.

Things were going fine with the scouts and with school. One day, however, Mr. Jones asked a favor, "I want you to take Eddie into your scout patrol."

Eddie Smith! He had to be kidding. Eddie was one of the toughest and roughest guys I'd ever known. He was trouble personified—a powerful athlete, a brawler, and just plain mean. The Mighty Jackson used to tease him. He would say that old Eddie was so evil that they could only bury him standing up.

Mr. Jones explained that Eddie needed acceptance. He also explained that the other patrol leaders had refused his request. So there we were—the Lone Pines at Camp J.K. Orr with Eddie Smith. Eddie decided that night to avenge a grudge against Frank Gaither. We tried to explain that the Gaither boys were not to be taken lightly. Eddie wouldn't listen. Two hours later, Eddie trudged into the cabin beaten to a pulp. It took another two hours to clean him up before he was presentable at assembly.

One weekend, the troop spent the night at the Trappist Monastery in Conyers, Georgia. Saturday night was a disaster. The Mighty Jackson, Bill Cannon, Black Bee and I were riding "borrowed" bikes to the grocery store when a car screeched to a halt, then turned around. We heard a voice screaming with glee, "Niggers!"

The car sped back in our direction. We steered our bikes down an embankment into the woods. When all was safe, we crept out to the side of the road. The bikes were severely damaged and we had some explaining to do. Meanwhile, Kurt Hill had thrown Arthur Micklebury through a wall back at the monastery. The following morning, Father Abbott thanked us for visiting with the Trappist Order. Tall and tranquil, he even invited us to come back. ". . . but not too soon."

CHAPTER VIII

St. Paul Remembered- Slight Return

If my memory serves me well, my formal education began at Ms. Scott's school located three houses north of the corner of Simpson Road and Ashby Street NW. At that corner was Charlie Sherman's filling station where our family, as well as that of many others, drove our cars for gasoline fill...Regular or Ethyl... oil refill and tire checks. Upon entering the third grade my mother transferred me to St. Paul of The Cross.

I was seated in the class of Sister John Vianney in the last seat of the first row in the classroom. To my left, seated in the second row at the last seat, was a brown skin beauty whose name was Karen Smith. Not only was I enthralled by her demeanor, I was also impressed by the way she used to curl her hand around a pen in order to write. I could not fathom exactly what she was doing at the time, but now I understand that she viewed writing in long-hand a/k/a cursive as an art form. Not only was I impressed with the beauty of her transcription, I was also impressed by the serenity that surrounded her as she put pen to paper. By contrast, my handwriting was so terrible that it paled by comparison. Shades of a future MD...No?

Sister John Vianney I think was the greatest influence on me at St. Paul as well as the best teacher I have ever had in life. In mathematics I knew how to do the work, but I never double checked my work. Therefore, many of my answers would be incorrect. Sister Vianney showed me how to double check my math and the light came on inside of my mind and I performed well thereafter. The message was clear; "Double check" is the key.

She also informed me I should stop using my fingers to count. I attempted to do this for a limited period of time, but thereafter realized I had trouble in dealing with adding and subtracting the numbers 9 and 7. Therefore, I would merely put my fingers behind my back and use them accordingly.

To this day I still have difficulty with the numbers 9 and 7. And if no one in authority is available to correct my methods, I do so openly and freely. Several months ago, I was reviewing a DVD on the topic of economics provided by The Teaching Company and during the course of the lecture, the economist freely counted on her fingers. I chuckled to myself and recalled the kindly yet disregarded advice given by Sister John Vianney.

But the biggest lesson I learned from the good sister was as follows: One of the first PTA meetings was up coming and at that meeting our respective parents would sit in our seats and review our papers. Sister John Vianney had us all accumulate our tests and assignment work along with their respective grades in a booklet form. Then on top of that she placed a hard copy of art paper and instructed each of us to write: "This is a reflection of me". Now wait a second. Admittedly my work was filled with a substandard assortment of A's, B's, C's, and D's. Thusly I proceeded to arrange the good grades and the bad grades in a fashion in which my mother, whom I knew had a short span of attention, would only rifle through the first few papers submitted.

But thereafter I really got the point that Sister John Vianney was trying to drive home. The point was that my work was in fact a reflection of my sense of industry and character. Keeping that in mind, I began to apply myself more strenuously so that the C's and D's were eliminated from top to bottom. As such there were only grades from A's to B's to review. As a practicing attorney who is required to write numerous memos, complaints, affidavits, and appellate briefs, I continuously revise and review my work after taking a pause, then cranking it up to a higher level. However, I still count on my fingers.

During the third year, Sister John Vianney asked me to give a presentation to the school on the life of Matthew Henson. I eagerly delved into the project and resorted to the Encyclopedia Britannica as my resource on the life of Henson, but also the life of Admiral Robert Peary. After delivering the dissertation to the entire school, I received much applause. As the various classes filed out, Ruth Reese walked up to me and said, "Gerald, did you say that Matthew Henson was black?" My response to her was, "Huh"? After all I was only in the third grade and really had no idea of the implications of the dissertation nor any notion as to the genius of Sister John Vianney in giving me that particular topic to deliver to my fellow schoolmates.

Fourth grade was pretty much a blur. The only thing I recall was the mutual agreement among most of our classmates that Sister Jean Michael was too pretty to have become a nun.

Our fifth-grade teacher was Sister Mildred Ildephonse. She was revered not only for her no nonsense approach to teaching, but also as a reasonably strict disciplinarian. Her favorite statement to us when we were misbehaving was, "I'll give you what Patty gave the drum". However, I cannot recall that she ever struck any of us physically. The most memorable event which I have told over and over in the fifth grade was the "KURT HILL ISSUE". Well I was seated in the middle row just in front of the desk of Sister Ildephonse. Kurt had done something bad which I cannot recall.

Therefore, Sister Ildephonse called for a vote. She asked for all those that thought that Kurt should be punished should raise their hand. Of course, I had no idea as to what Kurt had done one way or the other, but I was more interested in finding out if this was a true democracy or whether the good Sister really wanted rubber stamping. As most of the class raised their hands, I did not. Then when she asked all of those that think Kurt should not be punished, I raised my hand. Then the giggles began throughout the class.

I looked behind me and to the far left I saw Frank Booker and Obie Neal with both of their hands raised. Then I looked directly behind me and saw that Kurt was not only raising his hand, but was also standing upright. The entire class was having difficulty suppressing their laughter. "So, Mr. Yancey, you can now join Kurt and Frank and Obie in the back of the class in the last four seats".

During the rest of the year, Kurt, Obie and Frank took sheer delight in torturing me into laughter with their humor. In trying to suppress my laughter it came out as a high-pitched sound similar to something that could be written as "Aheet!" Everyday I went home with my side in stiches from the pain of laughter "Wow, what a punishment. I'll take that anytime".

Sister Martha Ruchin was our teacher in the sixth grade. A few memorable events occurred during that period. The first was when we were given an assignment in art class to do a poster on "vocations". I went home and discussed it with my mother and she informed me that the assignment was basically one that was exclusive only to religious vocations. That is, steps towards the priesthood or the nunnery, but did not include non-clergy vocations such as carpentry, plumbing, masonry, healthcare workers, physicians, etc. Therefore, I immediately lost interest in turning in the assignment and basically refused to do so. Sister Martha Ruchin gave me an "F" in art, of which I am still proud to have received as of this day.

The next encounter with Sister Martha Ruchin one where our sixth-grade choir was to perform in the balcony at the newly built St. Paul church at 9:00 a.m. I informed Sister that as we had divided up the altar boy service among various altar boys, it was my task, along with my brother Michael to service the 12:00 noon mass a/k/a the lazy people's mass. Sister informed me that I was to appear at 9:00 in any event. I could not fathom appearing at 9:00 and then having enough rest to service the 12:00 noon mass. Therefore, I did not show up. Naturally, I received another "F" in music, of which I am also proud of to this day.

As we attended Friday afternoon mass over at the St. Paul church, it was my task to take the keys to each classroom and make sure that they were locked up. On one occasion, I came across Ms. Phillips in the cafeteria who was the chief cook for the school. I became so enthralled with her persona and conversation that I completely forgot the fact that I was supposed to finish locking up, but at the same time, get back to the church for the service. For some reason Kurt was nearby. I have no idea why. But as I slowly came to my senses, I saw Sister Martha Ruchin climbing up the stairs in search of myself and Kurt. She was obviously angry and fit to be tied.

Kurt took off in one direction making a zig zag course back to the church but, I chose to stand my ground and not run. At the time however, I was eating a chocolate chip cookie that Ms. Phillips had given me and was slowly chewing it while waiting for the chiding that I knew I was going to receive from Sister Martha Ruchin. Immediately she asked me what I was chewing. I replied "a chocolate chip cookie". She then slapped me on the right side of my face with her right hand, and much to her chagrin, I swallowed the cookie.

Now that was not the last of my encounters with said Sister Martha Ruchin. At the end of the year, an awards ceremony was given for those that had made the Honor Roll. After the awards were given out, and as I was leaving the ceremonial area, Sister Martha Ruchin approached me and said you could have been on the honor roll, "like Tweet". Now I did not like the fact that she was trying to interpose my friendship with Tweet Williams as a way of making a point. I instantly knew that she was playing a head game, and I was not going to go along. My reply was simple, "I do not care". Then I walked away. As mother drove me home, she informed me that Sister Martha Ruchin expressed her anger at my cavalier attitude. When I informed my mother that Sister Martha Ruchin was merely playing a head game that I was not falling for she replied, "Oh, okay" and that was the end of that.

One similar event occurred in the seventh grade. Our teacher then was Sister Herman Joseph. I remember that I was studiously reading some text when I heard a commotion over to the far right where the doorway was located for entering and exiting the class. I saw Marty Bruce stand up and slap Sister Herman Joseph. I thought to myself, you can't do that to a nun! Then Sister Herman Joseph proceeded to give Marty a serious beat-down. Marty Bruce stood up, went to the exit, tore off the small fountain where the holy water was contained and threw it in the trash and stated "My momma told me I didn't have to take this shit". As expected, Marty never returned to St. Paul of the Cross.

Another encounter was one in which I went to Father Dennis's office and we had a conversation about the priesthood. I asked him if I could ever become a priest. He chuckled and stated, "No way, Gerald. Michael could become a priest. You'll only make it into heaven by the skin of your teeth". I replied, "Can I get that in writing, Father". He chuckled and pointed to the exit. Without hesitation, I departed. Future lawyer in the making...No?

Another event that I recall was when the upper class seventh and eighth graders went to a retreat at the Trappist Monastery. We were supposed to pray and reflect. However, being mischievous elementary school boys, we did everything except. At night the Mighty Jackson, Bill Cannon, Black Bee and myself, purloined some bicycles to drive up the street in Conyers, Georgia to go buy cookies at the grocery store. Along the way, a car rushed by, hit the brakes and someone inside screamed "Niggers"! I broke to the right and Jack, Bill and Black Bee broke to the left, each of us heading off into the woods.

Jack, Bill and Black Bee headed down a small ravine and I crashed my bike next the side of a tree. We all hid and watched the car back up and search around. But as we were hidden from view and it was night time, they could not find us. After they left, we gave up the idea of going to the store and walked our bikes back to the monastery and replaced them where they were. In the meantime, we had learned that a friendly row had arisen among the remainder of the group and Kurt picked up Arthur Mickelberry and threw him against the wall. The wall collapsed.

The next morning, Father Abbott, as he was saying goodbye to our class stated, "It was a pleasure to have you boys here and you are definitely welcome back...but not too soon".

I also recall the day that Mr. Jones, our scoutmaster, asked me to take into my patrol known as the lone pines, Eddie Smith as a member of my group. "Eddie Smith!" I proclaimed, I protested. I mean I had a great patrol. It consisted of Raymond "Tweet" Williams, Carl Barnes, Mike Gaines and I think Ed Thompson but, not Eddie Smith! Well,

Mr. Jones asked me to do it as a favor to him, so I complied. One day the troop went on a trip to Camp JK Orr for the weekend. Another group of kids were camped out as well. We played football against them one day. I think it was on a Saturday, and I found that they were much tougher and we went down in defeat.

There was good comradeship to go all around…for a while at least. As we were prepared to bed down, Eddie Smith and my patrol informed me that he was going to go over to the other group and challenge Frank Gaither to a boxing match. I probably informed Eddie that nobody messes with the Gaither boys, everybody in town knows that, but he was determined. We tried to talk him out of it. However, his blood was hot, for what reason I had no idea.

Approximately an hour later he returned bloody and bowed and as it was in the early morning there was soon to be inflammation. I attempted to arouse my patrol and help me clean up Eddie before we presented in formation. I think it was Mike Gaines and Carl Barnes who helped out immediately. So, we cleaned up Eddie and propped him up so as to be ready for morning inspection. We barely made it.

Perhaps the last fond memory I had of St. Paul was "The Great Race". Bill Bradley, The Mighty Jackson, Kurt Hill and Gregory Dinwiddie were the four legs of the four-forty relay. It was incredible. First Bill took off like a shot; cat quick and cunning. Then he handed off to the Mighty Jackson…poetry in motion. Jack handed off to Kurt who was the personification of pure determination. Then Kurt handed off to Greg who took off like the Flash. St. Paul beat the team handily.

However, we were playing in a South Georgia venue and it was very hot. When the afternoon came, the individual four-forty race was to be run. Greg our top runner was up against the other team's top runner. Come the afternoon Greg was fatigued and tired and lost to the other runner who clearly broke the finish line in an undisputable victory.

Deep down I knew that something was missing. I questioned Greg about the race and told him that he clearly could have beaten that other fellow. Greg agreed, but he could not figure out exactly what happened. Much later in life I realized that our team did not understand how to rehydrate and cool off for the hot weather. Not only did the other team understand the weather conditions, but also were more accustom to such.

Even though to this day I am not convinced about the "Theory of homefield advantage", but do realize that during that event… "The Great Race"…the south Georgia team really had the advantage as the latter four-forty race took place in the heat of the afternoon. In summary, there are countless other events I recall, but in the interest of brevity, have chosen only to recount those highlights stated above.

CHAPTER IX

From St. Paul to The Marist School

We were near graduation when I experienced two important phenomenon: the meaning of democracy and the opposite sex.

The meaning of democracy. Kurt Hill had been cutting up as usual. Sister Ildephonse instructed all who thought Kurt should be punished were to raise their hand. The majority of the class did so. Now I was seated in the first chair of the center row. So I couldn't really see behind me.

Next, she asked for a show of hands from those who thought Kurt should not be punished. Personally, I didn't care. Kurt was always being punished and to no avail. He was basically a good guy—physically powerful, aggressive, mischievous, but very loving and funny. Such an odd array of characteristics must be recognized and tempered.

So we were at the Ballot Box so to speak and to test the waters, I voted not to punish Kurt. The class howled with laughter. Slowly, I turned around to see the raised hands of my zaniest classmates—Frank Booker, Obbie Neal, and, of course, Kurt Hill.

I was punished by being seated at the back left of the class with the other three. I'm not so sure it was a punishment. For the entire year, I never laughed so hard in all my life.

So I learned the meaning of Democracy through a very undemocratic experience. Democracy means you can speak, write, or vote as you please without repercussion. Meaning no harm, the good Sister had just given the Bill of Rights a bad name. In America, we take things for granted, and that also is probably a very good thing.

The opposite sex. Ruth Reese was her name. I thought she was beautiful. She was raised by her father, Louie and her grandmother. Louie was an excellent eye doctor and spared me from total blindness years later.

Rust rings had formed on both eyes—probably after passing under a New York City construction site. He stripped and medicated the left eye first and then the right. Thank God for that man. My father had already gone blind. I had to care for my father and the blind can't care for the blind that well.

It was from Ruth that I received my first kiss in fourth grade. But in sixth grade, I found a letter written to my mom in the dresser at home. Ruth had professed her love for my brother, Michael! I stole that letter too.

Ruth and I were part of a debate in the eighth grade. Luckily enough, I overheard a conversation between mom and Ruth the day before. The topic had something to do with equal pay for women in the workforce. Ruth was planning to submit my own Mom's interview to bolster her argument!

Well, the debate raged on and then Ruth lays it on, "Mrs. Johnnie Yancey thinks . . ." The class howled with laughter, but I was prepared. As the laughter abated, I replied, "How would she know ? Mrs. Yancey has never worked a day in her life !" Even Ruth applauded.

The eighth grade was the year in which we all planned to go off in different directions. Even Sister Margaret Mary announced that she was leaving the convent to get married. I was to follow my brother Michael at Marist College. It was a Catholic prep school run by the Marist Fathers and retired Army personnel. It has since been renamed "The Marist School". I soon learned what it meant to have God and the state on the opposite side. My brother Mike integrated the school. Tweet Williams and I followed.

Father Brennan was the principal of Marist. At first, he didn't feel as though the school was quite ready for integration. Mom and Grandsir made an appointment with Bishop Francis Edward Hyland. She told me, "I couldn't do anything about Westminster or Lovett, but I'm Catholic and I could do something about Marist."

Years earlier, Grandsir was awarded a Medal of Honor from Pope John XXIII. The award was called Pro Ecclesia Et Pontifice which translates into For Church and Pope. It is an award conferred by the Pontiff for distinguished service to the Catholic Church by laity and clergy. The certificate itself is dated September 16, 1960. I think it was Bishop Hyland who actually placed the medal around Grandsir's neck in a ceremony over at St. Paul of the Cross. In any event, later on when Grandsir died, no one knew what to do with the medal. But Mom knew. At the wake, she removed the medal from its box, which was laying side by side Grandsir, placed it around his neck, and the medal remains with Grandsir to this day.

Grandsir received the award because years earlier he had convinced the church to alter its mission in regard to the education of Black Catholics. Religious conversion was fine, but we also needed mathematics, English, and science. The church complied and was amazed to see the Black children excel so highly.

When it came to Marist, Mom and Grandsir joined forces. Together they convinced God of their vision and the state complied. At the scheduled appointment Bishop Hyland took one look at Mike's test scores and called Father Brennan. Father Brennan agreed eventually. And under his leadership, Marist became the first Atlanta private school to desegregate. Mike graduated second or third in his class and was among the first of Marist graduates to go to Harvard. He'd also been accepted to MIT and Yale.

At that time, the Army ran the military and Mike was the Adjutant and third in command. He was the Chief Officer in the morning who called the main body to attention. Mike was sharp in his uniform— with the Sam Brown belt, sword at his left hip, and the all important officer's cap.

Years later, he confided in me that he hadn't enjoyed his years at Marist and did not care for the way his classmates denigrated people of color.

My first day was enlightening; I admit. Someone told a joke in ranks and everyone began to laugh. We were in B Company-Second Platoon. I laughed as well and soon found myself being choked at the neck by my captain who stated, "You little Nigger." It was then that I realized what it meant to have God and the state opposite me. It didn't take long to figure out how to manage them both.

You see, I had a secret weapon . . . Keith Spivey. Keith was to me as Pee Wee Reese was to Jackie Robinson. They would ask him why he would hang around with a Nigger. He would reply, "Because he's smarter than the rest of you".

It was Keith who kept me entertained for the next four years. We both were full of mischief. If you received more than 15 demerits, you would be discharged. I'd always managed to contain myself after 13 and then transform into an angel. For a given offense, it was noticed by my classmates that I would always receive more demerits for the same offense than the other kids. But that was put into the equation and never became a problem.

CHAPTER X

The Marist School Continued

After the choking event, I went to my first class. Who was my Algebra teacher other than Father Brennan? As he entered the class, he appeared slightly astonished. But mom had taught me earlier that Father Brennan was not a bad man. He was an excellent principal but somewhat dismayed and astonished by his place in history. Indeed that was true, and by the end of the year, he proudly placed an Algebra pin on my chest. The good Father nodded during the ceremony and even smiled. I'll never know whether he cared for me or not. But he did love mathematics.

It was Keith who drew up "The List" for me. Keith gave me the names of every student who did not care for blacks. One by one, I went about with my little plan.

If one of the members of The List was wrestling with a math problem, I would quickly scribble out the answer and leave my home telephone number. Persistence paid off and by the third year, a symphony of ex racists called my home for tutoring in mathematics, English, and the sciences. Johnnie thought it was hilarious.

Our geometry teacher, Father Gilroy, thought the whole thing was ludicrous, "Why do you bums all call on Yancey?" he asked.

Keith spoke up, "Because he can teach better than anyone else". Well, that was Keith.

I was intentionally bad sometimes though. Father Gilroy always went by the alphabet when asking questions. By the time he got to the letter "Y", I figured out the answer by process of elimination.

But when he wasn't following the usual order, I had to sharpen up a bit. Some days I would look out the window and act as if I was daydreaming. Boom! He would spring a question on me and in a sleepy monotone, I would deliver the proper response.

"Yancey, You're as crooked as the hind legs of a dog." he would state. I replied, "Dear Father . . . God made the dog's hind legs crooked so that he could run so fast."

In 1986, I revisited Marist and my dear Father Gilroy. He was very ill and we hugged. I reminded him of the hind leg story and he denied it: "You were a good boy and very bright."

I asked his driver, "Does it sound like him?"

The driver laughed, "It sounds like him." But Father continued to shake his head in denial.

Once Father Gilroy asked me what I thought of Martin Luther King, Jr. I replied that he was currently the greatest man in America. He and the rest of the class thought that I was daft. But I knew better. Johnnie told me so and they were no match for her.

Professor Juan Benedict, my Spanish teacher, was the kindest of all. He used to tell me that in Spain there was no racism. I guess he was being supportive. But I really had already figured out the deal and my plan had worked well so far. My greatest thanks goes out to him due to the quality of his teaching. Even now when I visit a Spanish speaking country, the quality of his efforts shows through.

I probably learned the most from Father Hughes however. Hughes didn't care for me that much. But that didn't matter. He knew how to write and from him I learned how to mix creativity and style with proper structure. I even learned at what point in a story I could stray from the rules.

One day we were given the assignment of writing a short story. I wrote about the sexual tension, timing, and misinterpretation between a man and a woman. The man was white. The woman was black. If you received an "A" you were allowed to read the story before the entire class. Hughes gave me an "A+". After class, I asked him why he didn't call on me to recite my story. He responded, "I'm just not sure about the morality of your tale."

Later on, we were given assigned topics for our senior thesis. They were marvelous assignments. Father Hughes was a brilliant man and the assignments ranged from topics based on the Iliad, Herodotus, Xenophon, Shakespeare, and Pericles. On the bulletin board I found my name and next to it was my assignment: "The Pastoral Elegy as Elucidated by Milton's Lycidas." He really didn't like me.

I carried my dilemma over to the Chairman of the English Department at Morehouse College. Dr. Jarrett was delighted and persuaded me that not only was this topic challenging but meaningful. Under Jarrett's expert guidance, I wrote my thesis. Jarrett made me do it over and over until he was satisfied. The good doctor once pronounced, "I won't rest until this is perfect." So for two months I wrote and Jarrett directed.

The assignments were turned in and several months later the grades were handed out. I was absent on that particular day. Keith called me around 5:00 p.m. He asked Father Hughes during class if the good Father had learned anything from the topics. Father Hughes replied, "Yes . . . one . . . The Pastoral Elegy as Elucidated by Milton's Lycidas."

I became an officer in my senior year by accident. The Air Force had replaced the Army and all assigned ranks would be re-evaluated. This was my chance to become an officer. Given my demerits, my assigned rank was no more than that of a Sergeant to the best of my recall. An examination was given, however, and the results of my testing had elevated me to the level of Captain. I was assigned to that rank as head of Company B-Second Platoon.

Mike was starting his first year at Harvard College. Labat was a junior at Morehouse at the time and Prentiss was at Howard University Law School. So mom's "little chicks" as she used to call us were all scattered about, yet learning and developing.

I did learn a good lesson in my senior year. I call this story *"My Favorite Beatdown"*. It all started in biology class. Joe Choquette, our instructor, experienced a disciplinary problem with the ninth graders that set him on edge. We seniors loved and respected him. As soon as we entered, he laid into us, "Take off those hats and sit down!"

Then I spoke up, "Mr. Choquette, just because the ninth graders were such a problem doesn't mean you can take it out on us."

Joe sent me to the library but I went home instead. Father Vedros was principal at the time and called my mother. He demanded that I apologize to Mr. Choquette the following day. The next day, I did apologize. No one in the class understood why. After all, I had only spoken the truth. Well, that was the problem. I had spoken the truth, but in my heart I was no more than a smart aleck. I knew it along with Father Vedros and Mr. Choquette even if no one else did.

Two months later, we were reading quietly during study hall. Father Emerick was a bright man and as strong as an ox. He slipped up behind me and with a clenched fist commenced to beat me on both sides of my neck.

Now at Marist, there were three basic rules. You never cry, never tattle, and never get caught. I didn't cry, but I felt like there should have been only two rules. One of my classmates, Joe Szabo said, "What did you do that for?"

Father Emerick replied, "Mr. Yancey knows." I did in fact and I deserved it as well. It was for the way I treated Joe Choquette.

CHAPTER XI

The Marist School
Redux-1963-1967

"Contrary to Popular Opinion the Initials After
My Name do not stand for send money"
Father James Hartnett, SM

It was a Friday afternoon when I met with Father James Hartnett to have lunch. We talked about the Marist School that existed during the period that I attended from 1963-1967. During that period Marist was all boys and all military. The military was based on the army model with a battalion commander, an adjutant, companies ranging from A-E with each company having two platoons consisting of approximately seven boys per squad. The common joke there as to freshman was, "Have you gone down to the armory and been measured for your rifle?" Of course, some would fall for it much to the dismay of the retired army sergeant quartermaster. Eventually he began to catch on to the joke and graciously informed the newcomer that there was really no need to do such.

Back then if you did something wrong you would receive demerits. If you reached fifteen demerits at the end of the year you would be expelled from school. As I was a black male, I often received more demerits for the same infraction than my white counter-parts. However, I did not let this deter me as after I counted and got to number thirteen, I changed into an angel until the end of the year. During my senior year the army model was replaced with the air force model. As I had received so many demerits under the army model, I was assigned the rank of a lowly sergeant. As I did not take the military aspect of Marist very seriously, it did not bother me very much. When the Air Force came in, the powers that be decided to reassess all rankings. We were given an exam. After taking the exam I received an A and was elevated from the rank of sergeant and made a captain. Surprisingly enough, my platoon was in Company B which was the exact same platoon that I was in when I first began.

I asked Father Hartnett as we wrapped up lunch why Marist changed from the military model over to dress code and admitted girls as well. He stated that they noted that the number of applications to Marist was dropping off along with the quality of applicants. Thus, after meeting with his fellow priests, it was decided Marist had to either stick to its guns and dissolve or change and reinvent itself. I asked him then what did they do about the military. He replied that military was optional. Thus the military applications dwindled down to nothing more than the flag bearers at football games.

I commented that when George H.W. Bush ran against Bill Clinton and H. Ross Perot that had President Bush taken the same tact, he would have replaced then Vice President, Dan Quayle with Colin Powell as his running mate. Had he done so, blacks would overwhelmingly have come over to the Republican Party in droves. However, President Bush stuck to his guns and as H. Ross Perot siphoned votes away from the Republican Party Bill Clinton became the newly elected President. In other words, unlike Marist, Bush stuck to his guns and dissolved. Whereas had he changed, and reinvented his cabinet, then no doubt he would have defeated President Clinton. Father Hartnett agreed.

ONE DAY IN THE LIFE

Our first class in the morning was usually in mathematics as that was when our minds were brightest and most clear. On this particular day during geometry class, Father Gilroy, out of the middle of nowhere stated, "Yancey! What do you think of this man Martin Luther King?"

I replied, "He's the greatest man in America today." I was jeered by my fellow classmates with boos and hisses which obviously indicated that my answer was absurd.

Father Gilroy then stated, "Why do you say that, Yancey?"

I replied, "Because my momma told me so."

My mother's maiden name was Clotilde Ouida Labat but her nickname was Johnnie. Prior to going to Marist, she gave me my marching orders. She told me that there would be racism. I would be treated inequitably. However, as part of the civil rights movement of the 60's, it was my job to make sure that I excelled in academics. Further, she and my grandfather, Arthur Henry Yancey, were instrumental in desegregating Marist. My brother Michael was one year ahead of me, and took exams at Woodward, Lovett, Marist and Westminster. He scored well above the 90th percentile in all entrance examinations; however none were prepared to desegregate at that time.

My mother then contacted my grandfather whom we called "Grandsir" and made an appointment to see Bishop Francis Edward Hylend. As my mother and Grandsir were highly influential in the black parish of St. Paul the Cross, they were able to obtain an interview with Bishop Hylend. Prior to that, Grandsir received an award from then Pope John XXIII which consisted of a certificate and a medal that was entitled the Pro Ecclesia Et Pontifice. My mom informed me that there was nothing they could do about Woodward, Lovett or Westminster, but being Catholic, there was something that they could do about Marist.

Bishop Hyland then contacted Father Vincent Brennan and asked him why my brother Michael was not being accepted. Father Brennan replied that like all the rest of the schools, they did not feel as though they were ready to accept colored students at that time. Bishop Hyland then overruled the good Father and insisted that Michael would be admitted into Marist. Father Brennan somewhat reluctantly complied.

But I digress. Returning to that day, lunch time followed two other courses, some time around 12:00 noon. I was standing across from the stairway in the cafeteria which consisted of two flights that lead down to the armory. Standing there I noted that one of the freshmen was sitting on the banister which seemed like quite a precarious situation to be in. Then I remembered that the eighth graders, being a raucous group always came through the front door, pushing, shoving and laughing. Suddenly I could see exactly what was going to happen. They were going to push and shove, and the poor fellow was going to be knocked over the banister down two flights of stairs and either break his neck or die.

The event seemed to occur in a split second and in slow motion. He was shoved over the railing and falling back towards his doom. Something inside compelled me to plow through the crowd, grab his lapels and snatch him back upward.

Now I cannot recall his name. But I do remember some six months later, I heard a voice inside the back seat of a car shouting, "Yancey, Yancey! Come meet my mom!" I leaned over from the passenger side and saw the boy's mother who was ready to drive him home. She took one look at me and her eyes were transfixed with disbelief. I do not think that she had any idea that a black man could have been responsible for preventing a horrendous fate that was in store for her beloved child.

That afternoon we had Father Hughes for both religion and English. That particular day Father Hughes handed out assignments for each student to write his senior thesis. While others received assignments such as "The Peloponnesian War" or "The writings of Mark Twain", I was assigned "The Pastoral Eulogy as Elucidated by Milton Lycidas." My best friend at that time was Keith Spivey. Keith was my Pee Wee Reese as I was his Jackie Robinson. Keith looked over at me and said, "I don't think he likes you."

After class I recalled reading Twain's "Pudd'nhead Wilson" when I was in elementary school and while taking a summer reading project at our local library located at the corner of Morris Brown Dr. and

Mosely...Now M. L. K. If you read ten books in the summer, you received a diploma. While I was lying on the floor reading Huck Finn, I noticed said novel. I reached up and began to read and concluded that it was the best thing that Twain had ever written. Yet very few knew about it as it involved slavery, interracial sex, murder, along with trial and punishment.

I politely asked Father Hughes prior to leaving the classroom why Marist students had never been assigned to read "Pudd'nhead Wilson". He replied, "Gerald, Marist students are not ready for that." Even to this day, I wonder if they are.

As for Milton's Lycidas, I went to my mom and asked her what to do with this topic. She sent me over to see Dr. Thomas Jarrett, the chairman of professor of English at Morehouse College. He exclaimed, "What an exquisite assignment!" I thought he was daft, but anyway, he told me how research is done in the English Department and he would make me write and rewrite my assignment using advanced English treatises along with their citations and that I would have to rewrite until I would have been granted an A to one of his graduate students. The first draft I wrote was horrible. The second was slightly better. After I wrote the third draft, I was beginning to get the hang of it. At the fourth draft I was beginning to get excited. Having completed the fifth draft, I turned it over to Professor Jarrett who stated that now I had the point, but was not satisfied yet.

Another draft followed and he said "There, you've done it." But I was not finished. I wrote a sixth draft and after that he told me, "Ok, Gerald... enough is enough!"

Many months later, our grades were posted and as I was sick that day, I called Keith and asked him how I had done. He told me that I received an A+. He also informed me that he asked Father Hughes if he had learned anything from any of the senior class theses. Father Hughes replied, "Yes... one. 'The Pastoral Eulogy as Elucidated by Milton's Lycidas."

Later that day, Father Hughes also held class in religion. I was always impressed by the fact that there was a corollary between religious doctrine, geometry and legal theory. In other words, you begin with a postulate, you have an answer to the postulate, but the work comes when filling in the middle. In religion class, I often dissented from different aspects of Catholic theology. For example, I could not understand why only a disciple of Christ could be admitted into heaven whereas practioners of Buddhism, Islam, Hinduism or even a Bantu or Aborigine could not. I further pointed out the confinement and harassment of Galileo by the Catholic Church for his hypothesis that the earth moved around the sun as opposed to vice versa. As such, his teachings were declared heretical and he was confined to house imprisonment until he died. The expression on his face naturally was one of disdain.

At the end of the day, we were in formation for dismissal. All of a sudden, we heard a loud blast while plumbs of black smoke emerged from the second floor. As the entire battalion surged forward, the officers held us back. Later on, we learned that Harry Weinberg, a very gifted student, was allowed to work in the chemistry lab alone after school. I am not sure, but I think that he accidently dropped a portion of potassium chloride into a vat of hydrochloric acid. Luckily enough, he was only burnt to a limited extent. The fascial singe gave him an appearance similar to that of a raccoon. Eventually, after approximately six months, his skin tone slowly returned to normal.

I was on my way home when I heard that there was a drag race to be held between Jimmy Bridges and Keith Spivey. The race was to occur beginning on the newly prepared 285 and was to end a quarter mile later under the Ashford-Dunwoody bridge. Jimmy drove a Pontiac GTO while Keith drove a Chevy Super Sport 442. Beau Means slowed down the meager traffic that existed at that time to a halt and then he gave the signal to begin the race. It was awesome. As it turns out Keith beat Jimmy by half a car length as they sped beneath the bridge. I then thought to myself, "Are all white people this crazy?"

Well, enough excitement for one day or so I thought. However, when I arrived home my mother informed me that Father Vedros, the Marist Principal called her and informed her that he thought that I was an atheist. Apparently, this was due to my earlier dissents in religion class with Father Hughes. I tried to explain, but my mother simply stated, "Gerald can't you just keep your big mouth shut. Grandsir and I worked very hard to get you into Marist!" "Oh well", "I thought."

Years later I was informed by one of my classmates, Dominick Sawyer, that Father Vedros left the Society of Mary, moved to Florida, got married and had children. Go figure.

Somewhere along the line, my good friend and fellow legal compatriot, Janise Miller, gave me a call. She asked that I write a recommendation to Marist for her son Brandyn. I replied that he would be better served if Michael wrote the letter instead.

THE SHEEP DOG

At the conclusion of lunch, I informed Father Hartnett of our first encounter at Marist when I entered as a freshman. I was taking his class in Latin and wrote my home work on my way home on the Oglethorpe bus line that carried me to downtown Atlanta. The next day I turned it in and as he rifled through the various assignments, he looked at mine and said, "This one looks like it was written on the bus." He laughed.

Some years ago, I was invited by Dr. Michael Bieze to speak to his Fine Arts class. I told them about some of the old days of Marist and then we went into a question-and-answer period. Among many of the questions I was asked, "What was the worst thing I experienced at Marist". I replied, "The food". Back then, it was terrible. You only had sodas, hot dogs, potato chips, and vending machines that were offered to you for lunch time. Eventually I learned to make my own lunch the night before.

Another question then arose. "How did Marist best prepare you to go to Georgetown?" I reflected a bit, and was reminded of a story I was told once, even though I did not know whether it was true or not. Essentially, I was informed that a sheep dog as a puppy is raised with sheep and therefore would herd sheep because he did not care that he was a dog. Well, I really do not know if that is true or not. But I do know that this much is true. I replied, "Basically I was just plain used to being around white folks and realized that they were not much different from blacks both with fine points and foibles. As such Marist best prepared me to go to Georgetown because while at Georgetown even though I was a minority I did not care that I was a minority all due to the Marist experience from 1963 to 1967 ".

My Grandmother used to say, "People are people". I did not know what she meant until now.

CHAPTER XII

Georgetown

Until Graduation, I spent most of my life either at Bay St. Louis or in Atlanta. Our home was located on Simpson Road where it intersected with Whitaker Road. There was a trolley stop at the corner and public transportation passed just outside our yard. The house was located on about four acres. We even had our own valley in the yard—an area we use to refer to as The Pit.

One day, mom, after much prodding, described her four sons again but in different terms. Prentiss was a blend of she and my father. Labat was much like her; they both had good hearts and hot tempers. Mike was almost totally like dad—mild mannered and benevolent.

"And who am I like, mom?" I asked in eager anticipation. "Well," she replied, "You aren't like anybody we know." A roar of laughter followed and being a good sport, I joined in with the merriment.

During my senior year at Marist, tragedy struck the family. One of Johnnie's brothers, Uncle Fabian and his son, Joseph, were drowned on a fishing trip in the Chesapeake Bay. Two others, the captain and his son, drowned as well.

My cousin, Dewitt, who had organized the trip, was the sole survivor. Unfortunately, he received the brunt of the family wrath. Mom argued that Dewitt should have been certain that all aboard were wearing life jackets. With the life vests secured, their fates would have been completely different.

Years later, I visited Dewitt in Arlington, Virginia. He was a delightful fellow! One morning, at my behest, we drove to Annapolis for brunch. At the end of our meal, he broached the subject of the drownings.

Mom had the story all wrong. Everyone on board had life vests. A squall blew toward the boat and swells were twenty feet high. The captain, for his own convenience, tied the anchor off the stern instead of off the bow as should have been done. Water was engulfing the boat and visibility was poor.

Any attempt to raise the anchor only caused more water to pour into the boat near the stern. Joe reassured his father: "Don't worry, dad. This boat is made of fiberglass. It won't sink."

But Uncle Fabian knew better.

"Boy, they have never built a boat yet that won't sink."

Dewitt then told me that the entire party abandoned ship with life vests on. He was the last to go overboard and he never saw the others again. But Dewitt had been a Navy man. In the Navy, he was taught to remove his life vest, stretch the jacket in front with one arm, and paddle with the other.

In this manner, he rode crest after crest until reaching the shore some four hours later. By wearing the vest, the others were pounded by the waves and drowned. Dewitt finished his tale as tears streamed from his eyes.

"And where did you embark from?" I asked. Dewitt pointed to a pier only sixty yards away. "From that dock right over there."

I promised then that I would do all that I could to set the record straight with the family. He thanked me and offered a swig of wine from his favorite little flask.

As graduation was approaching, my heart was set on attending the Georgetown University Walsh School of Foreign Service. The chain of events that followed my initial application could be described as truly ironic. In my reflection, I'm reminded of the events that surrounded the making of the movie, *J.F.K.* After the film was released, Garrison and his wife remarried. I don't really think she remarried her previous spouse. I think she married the actor who played his role, Kevin Costner—marriage by proxy.

I received at least two rejection letters from Georgetown. But Johnnie came up with a brilliant idea. She compiled a scrapbook of several achievements I had accomplished over eighteen years. Prentiss presented the book to Father Sullivan, the dean of admissions. The dean was so impressed with my brother that two weeks later, a letter of acceptance arrived for me. So I was going to Georgetown after all—admission by proxy. That's how I know about Mrs. Costner.

Loyola Hall was a residence for myself and many fellow classmates from whom I learned a great deal. Swifty introduced me to motorcycles. Larry Rohter hipped me to Muddy Waters and Jimi Hendrix, Moose Mallin loved Curtis Mayfield as well as King Curtis. David Giacalone showed me the power of genuine intent and the foolishness of guile. Rotten Richie taught me that everyone has a limit to what they can get away with. He should know. Richie was a cat burglar in the rough. His favorite trick was to climb the walls and peek in a class until spotted. His usual escape was through a nearby office window next door.

It was Richie who first solved the Cioffi problem. On Fridays, we returned from class and blasted our stereos in preparation for the weekend. Father Cioffi, who resided across the hall from me, couldn't stand the loud din of music. He often would burst in our rooms and confiscate our albums. But Richie had a plan.

One night he gift wrapped a box of manure and placed it before the Priest's door. On top of the box in an envelope he deposited a note. It read: "Give us our music back." The movers arrived shortly thereafter. The Cioffi problem was solved and we retrieved our music from his old room. We never asked Richie the source of the manure. We did have our suspicions however. Richie left Georgetown after his first year. He returned to finish as the rest of us were graduating. For the past three years he had been a cat burglar in Munich and had saved enough money to finish his education.

Professor Carol Quiggly was probably the most impressive figure during our first year at Georgetown. His course, The Evolution of

Civilization, still influences my thinking today. He was a dashing figure as he paced the stage of Gaston Hall while teaching his students the meaning of history.

Gaston Hall was beautiful, unique, and somewhat European. The walls were adorned with portraits of the Madonna and various artists and thinkers whom I never heard of. The carpet was plush red and a balcony hovered over the main floor in a semicircular fashion. Behind the stage, stood marble busts of Da Vinci, Galileo, Copernicus, and Newton.

Back at St. Paul someone asked the nuns why Christ was portrayed with olive skin, flowing locks, aquiline nose as well as a moustache and beard. We were told that this was the way people looked like at that time. That did not sit well with me. I could not imagine any person in our day who would be viewed as a representative of future generations.

At Georgetown Carol Quigley opined that as the early Christians did not represent their gods either in portrait or marble statue form. However the Greek Christians were in the habit of doing exactly the opposite. Thus the Greeks, being so impressed with the healing powers attributed to Christ, their portrayal of the Lord was based on their image Asclepius-a hero and god of medicine.

I don't know if this is really true or not, but much later in life during my studies at the University of Pennsylvania Medical School I decided to venture over to the Mutter Museum located at the College of Physicians of Philadelphia. Upon walking up the stairway towards the library I noticed at the base of a large statute the name Asclepius. I didn't think of it much at the time. However after a few hours study I descended the stairway and looked back. At that point I looked at the face of the statue of Asclepius. It's resemblance to our current portraits of Christ was uncanny.

Years later I got the idea to give a jazz recital in the Great Hall. I hitchhiked to New York City to retain Roland Kirk or possibly West Montgomery, but they were too expensive. At ABC records, I received a $1,000 offer on a new group that was up and coming. I listened to a few tracks of music, but concluded that if it wasn't jazz, it wasn't worthwhile, and therefore, passed on the deal. The group was called the Allman Brothers. Yikes!

A final contract was sealed with Lloyd McNeal. Gaston Hall was transformed that night. The idea took hold on other elements on campus and the Hall was often used for purposes other than teaching history.

During my second year at school, I grew lonely until I discovered Dianne Eagleton. She was a fellow student in economics that was taught by Professor Ibrahim Oweiss. At the end of the year, she ditched me for a Frenchman.

As fate would have it, Ibrahim was to become my lifelong friend and benefactor. He possessed an uncanny gift for seeing into the very souls of his students. I think it came from his religion. He was a Muslim.

One day Dianne and I were skipping class and drinking champagne in the courtyard with our zany friends in celebration of spring. The courtyard was encompassed by Loyola Hall, Xavier Hall as well as various offices and classrooms. David Giacalone went to the window and upon looking down onto the courtyard asked, "Professor Oweiss, can we cancel class and join Dianne and Gerry?"

The entire class slowly rose and peered down through the window. Ibrahim replied, "No, David. I don't think so." To this day, I still wish they had.

Eventually Ibrahim became an internationally renowned figure in the field of economics. For example as oil exporters settled sales in U.S. dollars the dollar became the most widely used currency. Thus it was easier for them to invest export proceeds in dollars. Accordingly, Ibrahim coined the commonly used term, "Petrodollar". He was also a founding member of the Center for Contemporary Arab Studies at Georgetown.

At some point in time Ibrahim called me to say, "Gerry, some man heard me speak on the Islamic religion while watching C-SPAN and requested an audience. His name is Muhammad Ali. Have you ever heard of this person?"

I chuckled and we both recalled the time when I gave him "The Autobiography of Malcom X" to read which he enjoyed immensely. So I found several VHS tapes on the life of "The Greatest" and mailed them to Ibrahim at his home in Kensington, Maryland.

A month later I called and inquired how the meeting went. He replied to say that at first he planned to invite ambassadors, professors, and other dignitaries to a luncheon. He changed his mind however and invited the neighborhood children instead. His home was inundated with kids from all around the neighborhood to meet and greet the great Muhammad Ali. Ali loved it! To this day I still wonder if the two got a chance to discuss the Islamic religion.

It was Pat Smith who recommended a job at the Cellar Door. The Old C.D. we used to call the club. It was more like a railroad car surrounded by brick masonry. Charlie Fitchman owned the place while Chris O'Connor managed. We were astounded by the musical genius that we were associating with on a one-to-one basis.

My job was waiting tables and my pockets were always bulging with dollars. I don't mind name-dropping when the names are worth mentioning. Among the many great acts, I can still recall: B.B. King, James Taylor, Bill Withers, Mort Sahl, Dick Gregory, Count Basie, Red Foxx, Olatungi, Miles Davis, and Richard Pryor. My all time favorite however was Uncle Dirty. Uncle who?

On Saturdays we would arrange softball games and the talent would join in the fun. Pryor was noticeably clumsy and would even dive at first base. No one dives at first base. I now think he had early signs of Multiple Sclerosis without anyone knowing it.

Miles loved to box and took a strong liking to O'Connor. He even invited Chris to jog and spar with him. Chris went jogging, but didn't want any part of Miles in the ring.

Prior to senior year, I was elected Chairman of the Black Student Alliance. My girlfriend was Dianne Watson. We used to call her Dr. Watson when teasing. Her father was Colonel Spann Watson-an original member of the Tuskegee Airmen. He would often chatter on about Benjamin O. Davis, Chappy James and A Train. We had no idea what he was talking about. Ouch! Also during that year I somehow managed to get arrested. Bad Luck Chuck and I were returning from a weekend in New York City. Chuck had an old German Lugar that he was planning to repair. The Jersey state police pulled us over for driving too slow and found the gun under the passenger side where I was seated.

We were arrested. Prentiss was livid but bailed us out after my call at 3:00 in the morning. I took the rap since Chuck had a wife, child and a previous conviction for teenage car theft. If tried he would probably have to spend a year in jail. According to plea bargaining, I would only receive one year probation. A few years later the record might be expunged. Never mind the fact that I was actually applying to law school at the time. Now it is no secret that a law graduate with a conviction might not be allowed to sit for the bar exam. Somehow I managed to put the issue far out of my mind.

On graduation day, Johnnie and dad came to see their youngest marching with his class. It would be of no use. A group of us were at The Tombs Bar and Grill drinking beer with our steak dinners. I left for a moment and found my parents standing in a crowd and straining to find me. So I peered along with them.

Mom spied me first and laughed heartily. Together we joined my friends at The Tombs and continued with the feast. I had been accepted to Harvard Law School and my friends and parents toasted to a promising career. Little did they know that my ambition did not rest with the practice of law.

Years earlier, I was advised by an educator and friend, Dr. Cleveland Dennard, to read "The Human Use of Human Beings." The book was written by Norbert Wiener. In one of the chapters, Wiener applied the laws of thermodynamics and information feedback to the legal and political arenas.

One day as I exited the front of the Walsh Building at Georgetown I thought to myself.. I am not smart enough to be a physicist, a mathematician or a chemist.. I got it.. I got it..I could become a doctor!" Thereafter it became my goal to obtain dual degrees in law and medicine.

In 1998, I revisited Georgetown. After making my way into the Doomsday Book office, I was allowed to glimpse through some old yearbooks. An editor inquired about Georgetown in the early 70's. More than anything, he wanted to know about the closing of the school and protest against the Vietnam War.

"We asked the administration about it," he began. "But all they tell us is that the school was closed and nothing more."

I proceeded to tell him of the events leading up to the closure and then of the votes that were submitted.

The editor motioned two other staff members over. It became apparent that what they found most interesting was the story of the balloting process itself. This tale I shall now relate to you.

A vote not to close the school had passed just before I entered the student government assembly. Kathy Sylvester, a friend and confidante, had cast the deciding vote. Asked by a member of the Assembly to state my point of view, I did.

"Harvard, Yale, and other schools around the country are closing to protest the Vietnam war. Why would Georgetown not take its rightful place in history?"

"But we have already voted not to close the school," responded one of the Assembly members.

I replied, "Then vote to have another vote."

A motion was made and seconded. The vote was tied again and Kathy was the lone remaining voter.

"What should I do? She inquired. "Let's close it, I replied." Kathy voted in favor of the motion. The new vote was taken and Kathy again being the last polled solemnly voted to close the joint down.

The faculty then followed our lead. Ibrahim informed me that he too had voted to close the school. He also told me that the Lauinger Library was built through funds donated by the parents of Joseph Mark Lauinger, who died in action in Vietnam.

CHAPTER XIII

Harvard Law

My First Day at Harvard Law was the second for my classmates. During what should have been the first day, I was in New Brunswick, New Jersey, replacing Bad Luck Chuck, for sentencing. Sometimes proxy knows no bounds.

Outside the courtroom, my law books were arranged on a table and I was busy taking notes on a legal pad. A member of the District Attorney's office became curious and asked me what I was doing. The bait had been taken. Now it was time for me to set the hook.

After explaining that I was in law school, he asked where I was studying. My matriculation card was handily turned over and the young D.A. was aghast with surprise. Fifteen minutes later, I was seated before the judge, the District Attorney, and my probation officer. After explaining why an innocent man had pled guilty, they reversed the conviction and set me free.

I was given one warning however. Never again was I, nor Bad Luck Chuck to be seen in the city. I quickly agreed. If you've been to New Brunswick, New Jersey, you would know how easily I kept my promise.

I rode back to Cambridge a free man on my Suzuki 500cc Murdercycle. After crossing the George Washington Bridge, a downpour of rain began. Soon I was soaked like a sponge, but there was no stopping. I could not miss another day of school. A normal four-hour trip took over eight hours. The rain ceased, of course, as soon as I arrived in Cambridge.

While asleep, a searing pain shot through both legs and feet. Some sixth sense prodded me to take a hot shower. After doing so, the pain subsided. My intuition was correct. The dye in my new blue jeans had penetrated the skin during the wet ride home. The hot shower rinsed the dye away. In the morning, Civil Procedure was the first class. Our teacher was Benny Kaplan a gifted copywright and civil procedure scholar. Our class was located in a large tiered room with plush green carpet. I did not know where my seat was, so I laid on the floor behind the last row of seats completely hidden from view of the professor.

As fate would have it, my name was the first called to recite the case of *Erie* v. *Tompkins*. How could I do this? I had just returned from New Brunswick New Jersey. Kaplan called my name again, but I refused to respond. Kaplan was befuddled. "Shades of things to come perhaps?" he mused, then passed on to call for the next student. That was my first day of law school.

I had two ambitions on arriving in Cambridge. The first was to go to law school. The second was to court Ann Brown, a girl I met five years earlier on a school trip of students from Cincinnati to Atlanta. Back then she dismissed me without a word. At Simmons College in nearby Boston, she was more receptive. After several attempts to be with her, she finally responded.

Law school classes were terribly boring. If I continued to attend, I would probably quit. So I decided to teach myself during the day and play basketball at night. I used this method during my entire stay in Cambridge. In retrospect, it was probably the best thing to do. Most of my friends to this day report a terrible experience at school. I had a blast, however.

During my first year, Johnnie was dying. She had contracted ovarian cancer. On one of my visits home, she confessed that she blamed my father for her disease. Apparently, she had multiple breast lumps and my father assured her that they were benign.

He was correct. But Mom reasoned that dad should have sent her to the Mayo Clinic in any event. There they would have detected the ovarian cancer. The notion, of course, was absurd. After reasoning with her, she finally realized her error. Eventually, she forgave my father for what he did not do.

Mom died near the end of the first year. I told her that whenever the sunset was crimson, I would pray and remember her. To this day, I still do.

Father Emerick, the deliverer of *My Favorite Beatdown*, attended my mom's wake along with Father Vedros.

Father Emerick inquired, "And, Gerald where are you now?"

I replied, "Harvard Law".

The good Father shook his head and stated, "I remember the day".

That summer, I toured Europe, visited Dianne and her Frenchman, and composed letters addressed to my father.

During the second year, two significant events occurred. The first was a bridge to medical school. The second was meeting Bill Mackey.

Larry Stephens walked up to my room one morning and knocked on the door. Earlier, we had discussed my ideas about the field of legal medicine. He reminded me that day of a conversation that I had long forgotten. Then he handed me a billboard notice obtained on a casual glance. The notice was actually an announcement of a new fellowship sponsored by the Cadbury Foundation. The money was to be used for pre-medical student education. After applying, I interviewed with Charlotte Cadbury, a most gracious lady, and was accepted. I was to attend Union College after my second year then return to law school to finish.

Now Bill Mackey was another matter. Ann was a dancer and invited me to a class; but I was more interested in basketball. One evening, we attended a dance recital where Mackey was the central figure.

He was a tall man, black as ebony, handsome, and slightly fearsome. His performance was magnificent and that evening I was determined to dance.

I really wasn't very good at first. Most of the dancers had started by age seven. How was I to catch up? It was not possible I concluded. I simply had to do my best and enjoy it. Later, Bill asked me to join the Henry Atlas Dance Company and I promptly accepted.

The Company was rehearsing a tribute to Billy Holiday and I was to play a small part in it. Henry Atlas was the founder of the Company that bore his name. His ex-wife, Consuelo, was retiring from the Alvin Ailey Company and would star as Billy Holiday. The concert was not well received by the critics but was instructive for me personally. Not only did I learn to dance, I also learned to think in a different direction—vertically.

Prior to this event, most of my conscious thought process was dedicated to linear thinking. A follows B in horizontal fashion. The process might be compared to filing papers alphabetically or even to planning and executing a career path. But with art, I learned to place A above B in a vertical fashion. This process might be compared to stacking pancakes or even to choreographing a dance performance or writing a novel.

After second year, most of my pre-medical training was done at Union College due to my benefactor, Charlotte Cadbury. Dr. Willard Roth, Chairman of Biology, served as a kind, generous, and patient advisor.

Biology was a lesson in vocabulary. Math was an art and the chalkboard was my canvas. My greatest difficulty was with organic chemistry—an exquisite science that required visualization of spatial relationships among carbon molecules. After numerous false starts, I realized that my high school science background was not sufficiently supportive. For my part, organic chemistry required understanding not mere memory. So I put off organic chemistry for the following summer to attend Harvard Summer School.

One year of organic chemistry was crushed into seven weeks! Our teacher was Professor Dan Sargent. He was excellent and expressed the opinion that if you could understand the helium atom, you could understand all of chemistry. Of further interest the good professor informed us that after writing the chemistry exams, the Chem. Dept. sent the questions over to the English Dept. for further refinement. The intent was that 95% of the class would interpret the exam questions in the same manner He also wished us good luck as a significant portion of the class would drop out.

Thereafter, I returned to law school to complete my training. The dean permitted eight credits of Physics from the nearby College to count toward the J.D. degree. Several weeks before graduating, I was accepted to the University of Pennsylvania School of Medicine. Dad came to graduation, but together we missed the ceremony. Beer and steak dinner were fine by us. I probably graduated somewhere close to the bottom among The Immortals. But so did General Grant.

CHAPTER XIV

My First Day at Law School

Many of you have asked what happened and that I tell the tale in more depth. Well, Bad Luck Chuck and I were working at the Cellar Door nightclub in D.C. when I was a Junior at Georgetown University. Redd Foxx was telling his classical story of "The Preacher and the Hunchback":

"The Lord made the heavens and the earth and declared that it was purrfect! Then the Lord created the plants and the animals and declared that it was purrfect! Then the Lord made men and women and declared that they were all purrfect!"

"Then a hunchback in the back of the parish asked, 'Well Mr. Preacherman why was I born as a hunchback?'"

"The preacher replied, you are the most purrfect hunchback that I done ever seen!"

Afterward he asked me to get him a glass of Coca Cola. I immediately complied and returned with a tall glass of Coke complete with a straw and as was the Cellar Door custom a cherry on top.

He gaped at the cherry with some consternation and as he removed it the audience howled with laughter.

"Oh. Think you are funny?" he stated. "Walking around the place with that big ass Afro lookin 'like an Ethiopian tryin' to throw spears at an Italian airplane." The audience howled a second time as I headed down the aisle toward the booth in utter confusion where Chuck was controlling sound and lighting.

Eventually Redd finished his last Saturday night performance and the staff began to escort the customers outside on an early Sunday morning. However one customer got drunk and planned to go home and shoot his wife. I opened his brief case, removed the bullets from his gun and placed them in my pocket. Chuck drove him home and put him to bed. I followed in Chuck's car.

Then we proceeded to New York City for a one-day weekend jaunt to the Big Apple. We arrived in New York sometime around 6 AM Sunday morning. As we were both in our early 20's neither was tired so we took in the usual tourist NYC sites via auto and basically just enjoyed each other's company. As dusk approached I contacted Marietta Dockery, a close friend of my parents, to say hello. She immediately invited us to a gumbo dinner at her high rise co-op on 125th Street in Manhattan.

Marietta's husband, Dr George Dockery, was a dentist and had many famous black celebrities among his clientele including Lena Horne, Arthur Mitchell of The Dance Theater of Harlem, and Thurgood Marshall. While Chuck and I chowed down an elderly gent seated to my left grunted with delight. "Um,Um, Um" with every spoonful of gumbo. In the meantime Marietta chattered on and on about "Cab" this and "Cab" that.

After awhile I inquired with muffled irritation," Cab who?"

"Why Cab Calloway", she replied.

"You know Cab Callway?"

"Uh yeah. He's sitting right next to you!"

I looked to my left at the elderly gent and asked, "Are you Cab Calloway?"

With a nod and a lift of his spoon he replied" Um, Um, Um"

Feeling utterly foolish I silently finished my gumbo. Then Chuck and I departed for the long road back to DC. After leaving New York City we were driving down the Jersey Turnpike back to D.C. We both got tired and pulled over on the side of the highway to sleep for awhile. Back in those days that is what you were taught to do rather than fall asleep at the wheel. Well, two New Jersey state troopers pulled up, woke us up, and told us there was a truck stop only a mile away and that we should go there.

We proceeded to drive off when I noticed that Chuck was driving at only 40 mph. I asked him why he was driving so slowly. He replied, in essence, that he was scared. When asked of what, he said that "His piece" was in the car and he was afraid the cops might find it. Piece of what? It turned out that he had an old German Lugar that he was repairing. It didn't even have a firing pin. And where was this "piece" I inquired. "Under your seat" he replied.

As you might have guessed the cops pulled us over for driving too slow, searched the car, found the gun, searched me and found the bullets I had removed from the gun of the guy who was going to shoot his wife. I forgot to toss them!

"Where did you pull the job?", one cop demanded.

"The job!" I replied? "We pulled a job!"

"So you admit it!", he replied.

"No.. I meant… We pulled a job! We pulled a job?"

That's as far as I got.

Immediately we were arrested and cuffed. I remember that night so vividly because I kept my hands warm on a cold January night, which were behind my back, on the headlights of the cop car. When asked by one of the cops what I was doing, I simply replied "Keeping my hands warm."

We were transported to the New Brunswick jail and while chained to a metal bench I stated to Chuck, "Now we are truly brothers". He gazed at me as if I had three heads.

Next we were getting our mug shots taken. I told the photographer my story and he thought it was funny. So funny that when asked if he would give us an extra copy for the folks back home, he complied. As we were being processed an officer indicated Chuck and stated, "I think this one should go upstairs".

At that point we both noted the lowering of a stairway from an upper area that seemed like a household attic from the exterior. Down it lumbered a huge white bull of a man that must have weighed well over

300 pounds and towered at least 6 feet three inches! As our eyes dilated, I grabbed Chuck by the arm and shouted, "That's OK Officer. He can come with me"! Immediately we both beat feet downstairs for the general population area where we found not only agreeable company but also checker boards, comic books and even plastic razors for shaving.

Being allowed one phone call, I tried to contact my eldest brother, Prentiss, who was a lawyer at the Smith Gambrell Law firm in Atlanta. His wife, Trish, informed me that he was away training in the Army Reserve unit based at Fort Bragg in North Carolina. She relayed my desperate need for $200.00 bail and by early morning he called the jail and asked why $200.00? I sheepishly replied a hundred for me and a hundred for Chuck. He was livid but sent the money anyway.

What finally happened? On the day of trial, it was 5 PM and our referred lawyer had not shown up. The Judge warned us that he had paperwork until 5:30 but after that he would proceed in any event. We were frightened. However at 5:15 PM a greasy haired, 5 foot 4 inch lawyer dressed in a rumpled black suit that appeared slept in with an American Flag on his left lapel burst into the courtroom.

"I'm Israel Michel your honor !", he started. "Sorry to be late but I am here to represent these boys" The bailiff could hardly hold back the laughter.

"Is that your lawyer?", he asked

"Oh God…I think so", I replied. "But he wasn't the one we hired"! And he was not. The lawyer we hired was too busy to attend that day and sent this crackpot in his place.

The bailiff just shook his head and slunk off to a corner of the room to snicker. Now we were even more frightened.

Chuck had a wife and kid and a past history of auto theft so I took the misdemeanor rap on a plea bargain arranged by our inglorious attorney. One year, probated and expungement of the record in three was the deal. I went back to D.C. and forgot all about it. Time passed and I was admitted to Harvard Law. Well guess what? My final hearing was scheduled for my first day of Law School. In other words when I was being sentenced everybody else was in class!

The fateful day arrived. I took my books with me to the Courthouse in New Brunswick, spread them out and pretended to study. One of the D.A.s became intrigued and asked what I was doing. I told him that I was studying as this was my first day of law school. When he asked where I was in Law School I knew I had him. I handed him my Harvard I.D. and watched his eyes dilate. He asked me what happened. I told him. He called the other D.A. over and I told him. The three of us went to my probation officer and I told him. The four of us went to the judge and I told him.

Long story short, the charges were dropped but the judge admonished, "Yancey, I never want you to see you in New Brunswick again". He also advised, "And next time you go to a courthouse do not wear a tank top". I took both pieces of advice.

And then…and then… And then as it turned out my conveyance of choice for this adventure was my 500 cc Honda Murdercycle. No problem except for the fact that once I hit the George Washington Bridge it began to rain. Thirty minutes later I was caught in a downpour and drenched to my underwear. But I just had to get back to Boston. After all it was my first day of Law School!

Upon arrival in Boston the rain stopped. "Free at last", I thought until my front tire landed in a pothole on Boylston Street . The water flew up in the air and I got splashed again.

Finally I dragged myself to bed in my dorm and fell into a deep slumber. But at 3 AM a searing pain engulfed my legs like I was on fire. Instinctively I headed for the hot showers seeking relief. It worked ! The rain had caused the dye from my brand new blue jeans to seep onto my skin! What a relief to rinse it off. I went back to bed.

That morning I attended my first class in Civil Procedure. I did not know where my seat was so I laid on the floor behind the back row. Professor Benny Kaplan spoke:" Mr. Yancey, recite the case of "Erie v. Tompkins" I didn't move a muscle or say a word. "Mr. Yancey… Mr. Yancey" I kept mum as everyone looked around.

I mean really. What was I going to do? Tell him about Redd Foxx and the story of the "Preacher and the Hunchback" along with the cherry… Bad Luck Chuck…the bullets …the gun…gumbo dinner with Cab

Calloway…the photograph… the bail relief…the imprisonment…Israel Michel…the plea…the murdercycle ride… the Boylston Pothole…the dye in my legs…never mind the fact that I barely escaped a conviction ? So I just laid there wrapped in the sweet arms of anonymity.

"Mr Yancey ? Mr Yancey ? Hum" Kaplan said. "Shades of things to come. Mr Jeffers." And that was my first day at law school or my second. Like a lot of things, it all depends on your point of view.

CHAPTER XV

Penn Med

After mom died, dad and I came closer together. Mike joined in and the three of us formed a ghostly trio. On one occasion, we were asked to leave the premises of a fine dining restaurant because of our dress. Mike sported a huge Afro-style haircut with a dappled tee-shirt and bell-bottom pants. Equally, under-affected, I was attired in blue jeans, a plaid pajama shirt and blue knit necktie. My father stated, "You two look like a couple of haints".

Finding ourselves outside the restaurant, the owner apologetically stated "We know you are fine people but we have to maintain our dress code". Mike exclaimed, "Don't' feel bad mister. We've been thrown out of better places than this." Even dad found the incident hilarious.

Johnnie told me that dad's biggest fear was of being placed in a nursing home when his time came. Even dad confirmed such one evening while chatting on our back porch. In that same conversation, he taught me a deep truth that he experienced in his own lifetime. He told me that a man must be physiologically prepared for failure in life. Soon enough, I would learn what he knew—not by logic but through experience.

On one occasion, after starting medical school, I called to express frustration over the complexity of the work. I was instructed by dad to throw my books out the window that evening and to see what happened in the morning. After doing so, I awakened the next day to see what had occurred. To my surprise, the books were still laying on top of the pavement. No one wanted my greatest treasure. The experience reminded me of my Uncle Vick's favorite joke: "If you want to hide your money, put it in a book."

Soon I realized that once again my science background was too limited to compete with the other students. My classmate John Yewdell made it simple. He put in one hour a night so I had to put in four. As he put in two hours over the weekend I had to put in eight. Eventually, I managed to pass all my classes during the first semester. Later on I learned that John graduated from Princeton University Magna Cum Laude.

Second semester, however, was a disaster. In fact, I somehow managed to flunk all four courses. The bar exam of the previous summer, first semester of medicine, a gloomy respite in damp New Orleans in January and new courses that required a deeper level of memorization were all contributing factors.

Biochemistry, microbiology, neuroanatomy, and behavioral science had defeated me and were the four walls of my prison cell. I stalked about campus, distraught and distracted until I spied a sign advertising the showing of an old feature movie. *High Noon* with Gary Cooper was playing in a few minutes. I purchased a ticket and waited for the film to begin.

Cooper was sheriff of the town and the outlaws were attacking. The townsmen were too cowardly to assist him and his deputy was drunk with jealousy over a shared lover. So Cooper did what any sane man would do. He ran.

His escape path was clear and lined by a seemingly endless row of trees. It was then that he envisioned an infinity of running and that he found infinity more frightening than the outlaws. So Cooper returned and took out the bad guys one by one.

The lesson was not lost on me. I spoke with my professors and arranged to take makeup exams in an orderly fashion. Luckily for me, the departments were scattered in communication. If one knew that I flunked all my courses, the story would be quite different. After succeeding in my second attempt, I finally completed the second semester—sometime before the third semester. During my next three years, I was able to continue with dance and took up Shotokan karate.

This practice of Shotokan was to extend for at least eight years in total. Our dojo was located on 45th Street in west Philadelphia. Sensei Teruyuki Okazaki was the founder of the East Coast Branch of the Japan Karate Association and when I wasn't occupied with medicine, I could usually be found at the karate club.

Karate had a profound and calming influence on my life. It was a constant in a sea of change. Designated hours for practice were sacrosanct and no distractions were tolerated. Like dad, Sensei one evening imparted wisdom from his life experiences to his pupils. Never allow money to guide your life's work. Do what you are here to do and the money will follow.

Of course, he didn't mean that money was not important. For my thinking, it is the very lifeblood of commerce. Never leave home without it, you might say. But the point he was making was that you'll be paid sufficiently if your work is valuable and true.

During the third semester, I decided to become a surgeon. Most students knew much earlier which path they were taking but I had not an inkling. We were sitting in conference and I reflected on what a happy experience I'd had with Dr. Alan Barr and Dr. George Dietrich, the chief members of the surgical team at Pennsylvania Hospital. A bolt of lightning flashed from the back of my skull to the front. So general surgery it would be. And so my life was to turn on an optical illusion.

At some time during third year, I took out three months to concentrate on Shotokan. The dean of students called me to his office and demanded an explanation. I would graduate with sufficient credits, I explained, and Shotokan provided something I needed to combine with my studies.

"Did you come here to learn medicine or to take karate lessons?" he stormed. The answer was obviously the former. "So why are you taking three months off?" he countered.

It was my turn, "Well, sir . . . because I like to fight!"

He laughed, then dismissed me with a wave of his hand. I was also instructed that he did not want to call me to his office again. That was not a problem, however. I hadn't forgotten Bad Luck Chuck or New Brunswick, New Jersey.

During my months off, I met Denise Quimby. Together we traveled to Tokyo, Japan and pushed further north to Sapporo then Hokkaido. In Hokkaido we lived in an old Buddhist monastery. There I continued my training and enjoyed the public baths and hospitality of the local townspeople.

On one day we went fishing with Joe Bogiesan in the Sea of Japan. We returned with enough flounder to feed the village. The village was animated on our return. It appeared that during our absence a young bear who could not find a suitable mate had trapped a citizen near a lake. The town physician seeing the event drove home to retrieve his gun, then shot the bear. A fish fry with bear meat was planned at the monastery for the whole town the following evening. Denise would also prepare a Japanese delicacy—homemade American apple pie.

Before the festivities, Joe Bogiesan invited me to his home for sake. We drank, then raided his wife's refrigerator and played cards. Time passed and in the middle of our merriment, we compared foot sizes sole to sole. It was then that Joe's wife entered to tell us how wonderful the festival was that we had forgotten about and how much she enjoyed the apple pie.

After my three months off, applications went out for residency. Much of my time as a student was spent at Presbyterian Hospital, where Dr. John Fobia and Dr. Gary Axelrad were senior residents. They wanted me to remain at Presbyterian, but I had broader designs. At least that is what I thought at the time.

One day an acceptance letter arrived from St. Vincent Hospital in Portland, Oregon. Portland was definitely what I wanted—a long high dive off the board away from East Coast living.

Dad used to say, "When Mike finishes training, he'll make a beeline for home. When Gerald finishes training, he will make a beeline for any place but home." A new adventure awaited. Many a mind pondered "Is Gerry ready for Portland"? Wiser minds on campus retorted, "Is Portland ready for Gerry"?

CHAPTER XVI

Forty Fifth St Dojo

As I finished my first year at Penn Med School, it was clear to me that now I had the time to take up an interest in martial arts. No doubt I was inspired by Bruce Lee in his various movie roles and as well as by David Carradine in the TV series "Kung Fu".

I first happened upon the Japan Karate Association Dojo located on 45th Street where I encountered an instructor by the name of Eugene McKnight. I asked him if they taught Kung Fu within. Eugene replied in a very haughty tone, "Here we teach Shotokan Karate!". At that point I thought to myself, "I'm not paying money to that ass". And so I continued in my pursuit of a place to practice martial arts. I then ventured to Upper Darby and found a facility that taught actual Kung Fu. It was an incredible sight to see. These guys were up and down, sideways, and back, sometimes with their bodies almost skimming along the floor and then poof upright in an instant. I inquired of one of the students exactly how the program worked.

He told me that it involved rigorous training and at the same time, that during a particular point of the year, that club actually went to China and fought from village to village in full combat. Being a fledgling medical student and not terribly interested in getting bloody, I had mixed feelings about joining the club. In any event, the main instructor, a chubby but robust looking Chinese man approached me and said, "You go… you go away from here!" I'm not sure what he was thinking. Perhaps he did not like the fact that I was of a darker hue than most of his students, but I really had no inclination to protest.

Thereafter, I found a karate studio somewhere around Broad Street and joined their group. However, I found that discipline was very lacking. There was too much socializing and talking and after two months I was the second-best karate practitioner. Concluding that this was a totally unsuitable place to learn martial arts, I went back to 45th Street. Upon entering I sat down with a different instructor, Ronnie Johnson, and had a discussion about Shotokan Karate. I was so impressed with his demeanor and character that I decided after watching a few classes that I was joining. And thus, began my commitment to develop myself physically, mentally and spiritually within the Japan Karate Association.

As such, I will only relay certain highlights as total recall would not only be overly broad, but also cumbersome as well. As stated earlier, Teruyuki Okazaki was chief instructor. Like most in our dojo, our first interest was kumite or fighting. But as time wore on, I became more and more involved and interested in kata or forms. What impressed me most about kata was the fact that I was heavily influenced around my immediately surrounding, fellow karate-kas. To be more precise, there was someone in front, someone to the left and someone to the right. Of course all of which would reverse when the full moves were in progress. But the fact was that their energies inspired me to greater performance.

For example, when Niles was in front, I was impressed by how low he could get to the floor, so I learned to train lower and lower and get closer to the floor. Faracchio… to my left… impressed me with his "C Step" and power punch and thus I was duly influenced almost by the process of osmosis. Giordano a/k/a "The One Armed Boxer" or as some might have it after he had busted them in the chest "The One Armed Bastard"… to my right…influenced me with his pure courage and determination. As such, my interest in punching and being punched in kumite began to wane and my enthusiasm for kata began to grow further. Kata was something that I could do at home, on the beach or even in the woods.

Well one-time during Saturday class, Tyrone was doing kata and someone from the neighborhood jumped over the banister and said "This karate stuff is bullshit!" Tyrone stepped forward and with one punch to the face, bloodied his nose and laid him out flat. Tyrone in dismay spread his arms, looked up at the ceiling, and exclaimed "This shit works!"

Another event was the shower caper involving Niles, Melinda Molin and myself. The boys were always in a race to get to the shower before the girls. Well the boys had less preparations to make and we'd always send one up to run in first and take the shower. The girls however, took longer preps to shower and they were always angered by the fact they had to wait for so many boys to finish so that they could take their showers as last in line. At one-point Niles and I were showering and Melinda just got sick and tired of it. So she stripped and took her shower with me and Niles with all three of us buck naked. We realized at that time that no one had any soap. So, Niles decided he would go over to McKnight's locker and borrow his bar of soap which turned out to be Irish Spring.

After placing it back, Sensei came out and wanted to know who had been using his bar of soap. Niles confessed that it was he who took it out of what he thought was McKnight's locker but it wasn't. The soap was taken accidently from Sensei's locker. So Niles informed Sensei that both Melinda and Yancey and himself had used his soap. Then Sensei confronted me, Melinda and Niles and says "Ah… all three of you must buy Sensei one complete box of Irish Spring and I want it by the next week". Personally, I thought it was so funny that I didn't really challenge it. The worst part about it was what it cost me. I think the cost was somewhere in the range of $25-$30. Well, $25-$30 when you are only making internship slave labor wages really hurts. We never repeated that mistake again.

Somewhat of a quandary arose within the Dojo concerning Ronnie Romano. Ronnie was a very fine karateka and I think he was trying to get his fourth dan belt. He took the exam repeatedly but for some strange reason Sensei wouldn't pass him. So one time I had a conversation among the other members of the Dojo and they couldn't figure it out either. They said from what they saw, Ronnie Romano was clearly head and shoulders among most of us and he clearly deserved to get the fourth dan. I had a conversation with Gerald Evans and asked him about it. He expressed his confusion just like everybody else. Then I said "Gerald, if Ronnie Romano doesn't make fourth dan, then what's the value of any of our belts?" Gerald replied "Good question Grasshopper".

Just before I was to begin my first year of residency at Presbyterian Hospital in general surgery my hands began to shake uncontrollably. I did not understand why. I went to visit with my cousin Herbert Nickens who was a very fine psychiatrist and asked him what was up. He told me it was a case of "anticipation anxiety". I did not quite understand what that meant and he explained. He opined that I was very anxious about starting my residency program. I said, well I don't feel anxious. He said, no you don't feel it consciously, but you are expressing it subconsciously. See how your hands are shaking and I said, "Ooook, now what do I do about this ?". So, I learned that I had a week between that day and start of my residency program and that karate summer camp was going on. I decided then to go to summer camp. Instantly my hands stopped shaking, I forgot all about everything as far as residency program goes, and I enjoyed the splendors of karate summer camp.

It was a magnificent event, with two classes of karate, one in the morning, and one in the evening, swimming, baseball, basketball and football in between. Now there was a known bar up the street about ¾ of a mile and Sensei told all of us to remember that we were there to go to karate camp and that we were not there to imbibe. After a good session of karate, sweating and showering, the next thing I wanted was something to eat and a cool beer.

Elaine Moyer, aka Nunu, myself and one other, ventured off and went to the bar somewhere in the late hours of the night As soon as we walked in we saw Sensei along with two other of the instructors... Mikami and Yaguchi...at the bar laughing heartily and drinking scotch. As soon as we walked in, they looked up at us and their body language and their facial expressions said, "You don't see us because we aren't here". We looked back at them, and our facial expressions and body language said "Ditto".

The last event I would like to relay took place just before I left Philadelphia to go to Syracuse to continue my pursuit of a career in general surgery. Apparently at the Penn School Karate Club after the end of a class taught by Gerald Evans, two practitioners were doing exactly what they were not supposed to do, that is, engaging in unfettered free sparring. Now this was a known no-no because it was too dangerous. However, one kicked the other somewhere in the mid-abdomen. Over time the one who was kicked dropped his blood pressure and began to pass out. Immediately he was taken over to Presbyterian Hospital and it could not be determined where he was bleeding from. He was given multiple transfusions and the doctors who examined him, even in spite of a normal nephrogram, decided to go ahead and remove his left kidney.

That did not do the trick and he continued to lose blood. I recalled that prior to residency during Med School I met a certain Dr. Alliva during my radiology rotation as a medical student. I watched him develop what he called the Alliva Technique. I asked him what that was, and he said it was a way of determining blood extravasation throughout the body by injecting technitium. So having recalled that, I suggested to my attendant surgeons that we send this particular fellow over to University Pennsylvania and allow Dr. Alliva to inject him with technitium and see if he could find the bleeding site.

As it turned out, it worked very well. The bleeding site was actually in a mesenteric vein that supplied the small bowel and apparently in the haste of doing exploratory surgery, the surgeons in charge had not thought to explore that particular area as it was such an unusual site for bleeding. The patient was reopened again and the bleeding was stopped and the patient did well. Gerald told me later on that the father of the patient gave him a very disapproving and ugly glance one time because he held Gerald accountable for what happened to his son. It wasn't Gerald's fault. The son, along with the fellow who kicked him, disobeyed the cardinal rule which is never engage in free unfettered sparring outside of the direction and control of your karate instructor.

CHAPTER XVII

That Boy Needs a Dog

Ever since childhood, I always had a dog. In fact, we had so many dogs that either ran away, died, or got run over that Labat would say, "They're not dogs, Gerald, they're victims!" But whenever we lost one, Grandma would find a replacement somewhere and send him over to Simpson Road.

Johnnie would get infuriated, but Grandma would insist; "That a boy needs a dog!" Mom's favorite was Waggy, the one who helped me survive the vicious assault of The Black Dog. My favorite was Gandalf for he survived living with me for at least eleven years.

My good friend Loretto Grier and I chose Gandalf at a pound one rainy night in Philadelphia. Actually, he was a replacement for the mighty collie, Moses Rose, that had skipped away from a neighbor's control.

It was Gandalf, another collie, who accompanied me on the trip to Portland. Shortly after our arrival, I was completely unable to find an apartment that would allow animals. My father advised that Gandalf be surrendered to the pound so that I could begin residency on time.

En route to the animal shelter, I felt like Abraham preparing Isaac for the slaughter. But rebellion overtook me and after deciding that: "God didn't tell me to do this," I changed my mind. I also resigned my position.

After calling back to Philadelphia, Dr. John Fobia and Dr. Gary Axelrad obtained a position for me at Presbyterian. The problem was that I could not begin until the following year.

While traveling back to Philadelphia, I noticed a crimson sunset and thought about Johnnie. It wasn't the first time, of course, but the occasion was different. Not only did I remember Mom fondly, but also began to reinterpret the experience. It had become a sign of approval.

Upon return to Philadelphia, I had no idea what to do for a year. Prentiss hoped I had learned a lesson. Labat thought the whole event hilarious. Mike believed there was method to my madness, but dad was furious as was the chief surgeon at St. Vincent. He and Johnnie had spent so much hope and energy in our development. How could I play Ricochet Romance so recklessly? Ibrahim opined, "Only you would risk your career for a dog". But Grandma said it long ago: "That boy needs a dog".

One day after karate class, an excellent idea dawned. I would visit The Master. Robert Johnson was a brilliant anatomist at the medical school. I had taken several advanced courses under his tutelage as a student. Perhaps he would allow me to advance my studies in Anatomy under his supervision.

Johnson consented and even provided an office, teaching duties, and a position as Post Doctorate Fellow. I was never sure if he made the latter up, but it did come with a meal card and a membership to the gymnasium. I loved that man.

That year was the springtime of my life. My health was at its peak. I could continue training in Shotokan, then dissect cadavers well into the night. However I realized that it was not going to last.

I began surgical residency the following year and spent two years at Presbyterian Hospital. During this period, I was transformed into a doctor by a singular event. I was by most standards a mediocre intern— more interested in leaving the hospital on time than in my mission. Early second year, I was called to see a patient five minutes before shift change. The patient was an elderly black male who complained of shortness of breath. Upon arrival, he looked exhausted but assured the staff that he was not in distress. I received this news with relief and was reassured by the nurses as well. So I departed. But on the ride home, some sixth sense haunted me.

Arriving home to my row house on Abbotsford Road, I called Axelrad and related the experience. I was told that the patient was dead. He had suffered a pulmonary embolism and ceased breathing shortly after my departure from the hospital. Axelrad gave his assurances that I was not at fault; but I knew better. The sixth sense was an afterthought only. Unless it could be encapsulated as an integral part of my personality, I would have to resign.

Now there was a small park nearby located at the intersection of Germantown Avenue and Abbottsford Road. There I laid prostrate, face down in the grass, determined not to get up until my dilemma was solved. Nearly four hours elapsed until I arose, like Antaeus, renewed and resolved. The problem was the answer and vice versa—time management.

My own pleasures could not be resisted. But my duties could not be ignored. After several hours of consideration, my life was reorganized along these principles. After shift change, I learned to spend an extra hour for emergencies, additional learning, and review of the patients. This was followed by dinner, an hour and a half of exercise, then I would return to the hospital.

During the latter period, time was spent reviewing and fine-tuning patient care. This new approach astounded everyone, including myself. I even dedicated Thursday evening to socializing with my patients— sipping wine, playing poker for quarters, or discussing politics.

That year, Presbyterian was overloaded with general surgeons. In spite of the conversion, I wouldn't be chosen among four residents for one of two positions. So I transferred to a different hospital—St. Ambrose in Syracuse, New York. In Syracuse, unbeknownst to me, I was to face a terrible phenomenon—Death in Tehran.

CHAPTER XVIII

Death in Tehran

Before she died, Johnnie expressed her concerns one afternoon on the ride home after chemotherapy. She worried about Prentiss with his trusting nature, Labat with his career, and Mike, after two car accidents, with his driving. She wasn't worried about me though. Somehow, I felt left out. In Syracuse, I learned that worry would be wasted on me. I was doomed.

The tale goes that the King and Death were talking in the palace when the young Lord arrived. Seeing Death, the Lord saddled his horse and left in fear on a two-day ride to Tehran. Death was surprised as well. When the King asked why, Death responded, "Because I am supposed to take that Young Lord in Tehran two days from now." At least half a year elapsed in Syracuse before Death found me.

After several months at St. Ambrose, the In-Service Exam was given to measure the knowledge of the surgical residents. I realized this exam would be used not merely as a barometer but as a final test for career advancement. Surgeons were too numerous and programs were being closed throughout the nation. How well the residents performed on the In-Service Exam would determine the fate of a particular program. Several purloined exams were offered to me. I was warned by several residents that without them there would be no hope. It would be like racing in the Tour De France without steroids. Yet, I had resolved years earlier that failing was better than academic dishonesty. The exam was given and after several weeks, the results were back. My results were a dismal 25 percent.

The Chief of Surgery was enraged. I would have to repeat a year if I was to stay in the program. I politely but firmly refused. I could not bring myself to "rat" on the other guys. I could have used my legal skills to invalidate the exam but that would entail harming the reputation of a lot of people including St. Ambrose. So in a flash, I knew my dream of becoming a surgeon was irrevocably shattered. From the palace to Tehran or from Philadelphia to Syracuse, Death found me where I belonged.

Two weeks later I was confronted by a fellow resident, Bob Nicase, who asked of my plans. Responding that funerals and wakes were not my strong points, Bob gently led the way to the hospital library. There, through journals and job advertisements, he demonstrated that I was merely the victim of supply and demand. The future was in the field of Family Practice and the supply was minimal. God bless that man. So I determined that I would combine teaching anatomy with three years of general surgery and three years of family practice and become an ER doctor.

So I learned that there was life after surgery. Resurrection began and three years later I completed the St. Clare's Hospital Family Practice Program in Schenectady, NY. From Schenectady I ventured back home to Atlanta. A long and arduous odyssey finally came to an end.

Just before graduation, however, I realized that dad was dying. He had been weak for several years after an operation. It was my habit to call from time to time to encourage him. But this call was different. While talking on the line, I received no response. He had fallen.

Years earlier he would tell me that if I came home, he would give me his medical practice. I politely refused, but promised to write semi-regularly from some far and distant land. We talked again—the day after the fall. Once again, he asked that I come home. He was lonely.

I arrived in Atlanta and obtained a position at South Fulton Hospital as an Emergency Room Physician. I even managed to open a consulting firm in legal-medical issues both civil and criminal. Prentiss, by then, was a senior partner at the law firm of Smith Gambrell. Labat was a Vice President at Equifax. Mike became a neurosurgeon and was employed at Arnot Ogden Hospital in Elmira, NY. Dad was diagnosed with Shy-Drager Syndrome which is a condition that causes the blood pressure to drop upon standing. As such he was confined to bed. He died peacefully one Monday morning at his home on Simpson Road.

Before his death, I inquired about the small horizontal scar on his lower right abdomen. How did this happen? He explained.

Dad was born to be a physician. Yet he had no knowledge of what it was like to be a patient. So one day, after reading about appendicitis, dad told Grandsir about pain in his right lower side. The whole thing was merely a ruse. Several days later, he returned home triumphantly from the hospital without a normal appendix. From this experience, dad learned a most valuable lesson which then was imparted to me; "It's better to be the doctor, son, than to be the patient."

One day a group of us decided to visit my uncle, Asa G. Yancey, MD at his home on Engle Road in Atlanta. Asa was a highly gifted surgeon who prior to retirement served as the first black Medical Director at Grady Hospital. As he was also a good friend of Dr. Charles Drew, a highly noted researcher and developer of blood storage and preservation during World War II, we inquired about the death of Dr. Drew in 1950.

According to popular myth after a car accident Dr. Drew was denied a blood transfusion, the very work in which he had endeavored, at Alamance General Hospital located in Burlington, North Carolina because of the color of his skin. Asa informed us that this was not the case and that Dr. Drew's injuries were so severe that even a blood transfusion would not have saved his life.

A year before dad's death, the disease struck. My body was racked with misery. Antibodies were attacking the nervous system and once proud muscles lay atrophied, in waste and replaced by scar tissue due to a rare condition called Lambert-Eaton Syndrome. Like Rodney Dangerfield, I was resigned to donating my body to science-fiction.

Elizabeth, my new wife, suggested travel as distraction and partly as therapy.

Her lifelong friend, Rudy Tucker, had a son who was a fisherman. I met with Stefan and together we planned our trip to Bob's Fishing Paradise in Placencia, Belize. From Placencia, we could fish and tour the countryside. A side trip to Guatemala might even be arranged.

It was around sunset when the taxi arrived. The driver was gracious in lending assistance as I struggled to lift my gear. En route to the airport, the cabby spoke cheerfully of his life and his losses. The sunset was crimson and I thought of Johnnie.

CHAPTER XIX

Flashback-No Rest for the Wicked

It was a Friday afternoon in Schenectady. I was only two hours shy of completing my rotation in Psychiatry at St. Clare's Hospital Family Practice Program.

I was sitting in the corridor and noticed that no one was paying me any attention. So why not be just a little wicked …..and split early ? So, I did.

On State St. I entered the local bank to make a withdrawal. I soon spotted an elderly gentleman napping quietly upright on a couch. Slowly he began to keel over, and my Lord, he was turning blue!

Almost instinctively I laid him flat on the floor and began to administer CPR. "911"! I shouted! Was that my voice in between nearly every breath? The ambulance arrived and as they administered oxygen using a bag and mask he began to "pink up". Then I began to rifle through his personal belongings while the EMTs began loading him on a gurney.

Perhaps I could find an ID and notify the family. After going through numerous papers, which I promptly through over my shoulder, I finally found an identification card. His name was John Vescucci. I gave the ID to the emergency team, and continued to go on with the business of banking. Later, I learned that John had been admitted to the ICU at St. Clare's with the diagnosis of congestive heart failure, and was doing very well . Before he was sent upstairs, he asked the nurses to call me to room 16 in the Intensive Care Unit.

"Dr. Yancey" he began, "I want to thank you for just having been there in the nick of time".

"No problem", I replied, while deep down I knew I was supposed to be in the Psychiatric Ward, but I was being wicked.

"I just wanted to know if perhaps they found some papers among my belongings".

"Well, John, there were some funny looking papers with a lot of blue ink".

"Dr. Yancey – those were three bonds that were worth $25,000 each".

"Well take it easy John. After all, I did save your life".

Dejected, John looked down and replied "So what's my life without my money?"

He did have point. So I went over to the nursing station and called the bank and learned that the bonds were in its possession as the employees had retrieved them off the floor and the bank was holding them for safe keeping. I informed John as such.

"Dr. Yancey! You saved my life, twice!"

Okie dokie. So John went "upstairs" for a few days of rest before being discharged. However, one of the ICU Attendees inquired, "Hey Yance, weren't you supposed to be in Psych at that time?"

I excused myself for a bathroom break, but never returned to the scene.

A few days later while busily pursuing my tasks back at the ICU a nurse shouted "Room 16...V Fib !" Room 16 was John's old room, and I was right in front of it. I looked over and saw a 50 year old male slumped in his bed, and unconscious.

As the nurses gathered up the crash cart, I decided to try a Pre Cordial Thump. Holding my right fist back, I struck down in hammer – like fashion over the left chest. It worked! The heart rate corrected to normal sinus rhythm. We bolused him with Licocaine and started an intravenous drip. I walked on.

A few days later the hospital operator summoned me to the room of John Vescussi. John was scheduled for discharge.

"Dr. Yancey" he began, "I got a little gift for you". Oh boy … what could it be? I learned over the past week that John had earned a fortune in the Venetian blind business. John Vescucci, in fact, was wealthy, even if by Schenectady standards. Could I take money? I did have an eye on a Crimson Honda 1250 cc Aspencade Murdercycle.

John reached into his pocket and pulled out what appeared to be a small leather case. Inside the case was a small metal device with multiple appendages.

"Dr. Yancey, I just love this thing. Here … see? You can cut your nails, and with this you can even trim and file".

I stopped listening. No Honda Aspencade was forthcoming for me. Well … I feigned gratitude and wished John the best of health. After that I returned to my duties in the ICU. One day, along came the attending for Pre Cordial Thump Man. He was laughing over and over.

"Yance, remember that guy that you gave a Pre Cordial Thump to a few days ago?"

"Ahhh… yeah!"

"Well he wants to know who was that black bastard who hit him in the chest".

Oh well…No rest for the wicked.

EPILOGUE

Many men think that a man's enemy is another man. Men make enemies of each other. I guess that is true. But mankind has another and perhaps even greater enemy it must face-disease and pestilence. Stated differently, man's worse fate is creation.

The age-old question simply boils down to whether it is better to be born or not to be born. I suppose everyone must decide that for himself. The greatest wonder of all, though, is that death is all around us, yet we behave as if death does not exist.

I have spent much of this short narrative speaking about the woman who brought me to this earth. I was once warned in life that we must be careful how we treat the dead; for they are not present to defend themselves. I hope that I have treated my mom with warmth and compassion. Like a constellation that has dropped beneath the horizon, I can no longer see her. Yet she is still with me.

Today I returned to Placencia. After a successful week of fishing, Stefan has gone back to work and Sonny has returned to his family in Monkey River Village. I look out at the harbor and see the boats coming in and the cars passing by the waterfront. I'm doing my best to answer the age-old question for myself. But last night on a boat ride back to port, I experienced a small revelation. Mom had chosen me to be the first to suffer and perhaps the first to die. If this was truly the case, then wouldn't I also be the first to go home?

PHOTO GALLERY

Johnnie and her four Chicks
Lt to Rt: Prentiss, Labat, Michael
and Gerald

Johnnie and Michael

Dr. Prentiss Q. Yancey

Farther Emmanuel Trainer

Sisters of St. Joseph
Top Lt to Rt: Sister John Vianney,
Sister Martha
lldephonse and
Sister Jean Michael
Bottom Lt to Rt:
Sister Noel and Sister Malcolm

St. Paul of the Cross Catholic Elementary School
551 Harwell Road
Atlanta, Georgia 30318
6th Grade
Red Step Picture

Boys (Top step/Lt to Rt)

1. Bernard DuBose
2. Gerald Yancey
3. Michael Jenkins
4. William Bradley
5. Arthur Emory
6. Kurt Hill
7. Reginald Lopez
8. Gregory Dinwiddie
9. Ellis Farrell
10. Arthur Jackson
11. Frank Booker
12. Angus Stevenson
13. Lafayeffe Sherman
14. James Williams
15. Edward Bowen
16. Obie Neal

Girls (Bottom step/ Lt to Rt)

1. Rita Robinson
2. Pamela Jackson
3. Carolyn Barr
4. Peggy Hall
5. Regina Hardy
6. Paula Wilson
7. Karen Smith
8. Angelyn Couch
9. Ruth Reese
10. Neeka Milsap
11. Dorothy Brown
12. Berneda Johnson
13. Amaryllis Grogan
14. Sundra Burdett
15. Reginia Rogers
16. Gail Marigny
17. Kathy McCree
18. Claudia George

Sister Jean Michael

Johnnie and Dr. Prentiss Q. Yancey
awarding the Eagle
Scout Pin to Gerald and Michael

Scouts from Troup 383 Receive
the Ad Altare Dei Award
Top Lt to Rt: Father Christidh, Michael Yancey, James
George, Scout Master Milton Jones and Andrew Hill
Bottom Lt to Rt: James Williams and Gerald Yancey

Archbishop awarding Lost Ad Altare
Dei Award Ceremony
Lt to Rt: Gerald Yancey, Attorney Janise Miller,
Archbishop Wilton Gregory and Michael Yancey

The Pro Ecclesia Et Pontifice awarded
to Arthur H. Yancey
by Pope John XXIII

IOANNES XXIII PONTIFEX MAXIMVS

AVGVSTÆ CRVCIS INSIGNE

PRO ECCLESIA ET PONTIFICE

EXIMIAM PONENTIBVS OPERAM PRÆCIPVE CONSTITVTVM

D.no Arturo D. Yancey

DECERNERE AC DILARGIRI DIGNATVS EST, EIDEM PARITER FACVLTATEM

FACIENS SESE HOC ORNAMENTO DECORANDI

EX ÆDIBVS VATICANIS, DIE 16 Septembris 1960

Home of Arthur H. Yancey I 636 Beckwith St.
Atlanta, Georgia

Kareem Oweiss Sparring With Muhammad Ali

In Celebration of 100 Years of Celestine "Aunt Tennie" Labat
Lt to Rt: Dr Joseph Labat, Joseph "Teddie Boy" Labat Ernestine Labat, Rudy Labat, Ce lestine "Aunt Tennie" Labdt, Victor Labat, Labat Yancey and Michael Labat

Jailbird...My First Day at Law School

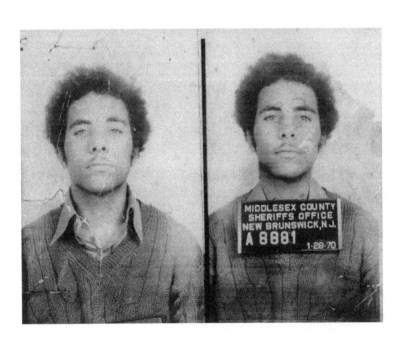

The Author at the Forty Fifth St. Dojo

Calligraphy from Sensei Masatoshi Nakayama to
Christopher Giordano
Internal Peace through Training

Calligraphy from Sensei Masatoshi Nakayama to
Christopher Giordano
Repetition... Meditation

Doctor Asa G. Yancey

GANDALF

Fishing in Belize